The New Testament Church Book

An Anthology of
Teaching and Example

Compiled and Edited by Al West

Illustrations by Steve Crain

LOGOS INTERNATIONAL
Plainfield, New Jersey

THE NEW TESTAMENT CHURCH BOOK
© 1973 by
Logos International Inc.
Plainfield, New Jersey
07060
Printed in the United States of America
P-045

INTERNATIONAL STANDARD BOOK NUMBER   0-88270-045-6

Contents

The New Testament Church

And those who believed Peter were baptized—about 3,000 in all! They joined with the other believers in regular attendance at the apostles' teaching sessions and at the Communion services and prayer meetings. A deep sense of awe was on them all, and the apostles did many miracles.

And all the believers met together constantly and shared everything with each other, selling their possessions and dividing with those in need. They worshipped together regularly at the Temple each day, met in small groups in homes for Communion, and shared their meals with great joy and thankfulness, praising God. The whole city was favorable to them, and each day God added to them all who were being saved.

Acts 2: 41-47 The Living Bible

Introduction

An Episcopal priest some years ago startled his congregation by reporting he had undergone the same experience as the apostles on the day of Pentecost. The claim was so extraordinary for that decade and situation that it made secular headlines in newspapers and magazines. The generally accepted notion was that such an experience had not occurred for nearly 2,000 years. Nothing was further from the truth, of course, Pentecost was alive and well even though shoved beneath a bushel.

For most of the 20th century, the pentecostal experience had not been accepted as a reality by institutional Christianity as a whole, except in the so-called Pentecostal denominations. The latter had arisen with the onset and assimilation of a theory called dispensationalism. That still prevalent institutional doctrine holds that the power and gifts of the Holy Spirit disappeared from the earth when the last of the original apostles died. Consequently, during the first 60 years of this century the Holy Spirit was relegated to a more symbolic than literal role; and the practices and ordinances of the early church—the church of the New Testament—passed into relative obscurity.

No wonder so many people were shaken by the bold pronouncement of that Califonria priest. In actuality, he had "fallen in" with some Pentecostals and received God's promises as contained in the Scriptures.

Tens of thousands of seeking Christians have since entered into the same spiritual state and an outpouring of the Holy Spirit is sweeping the world as never before. Hardly a segment of Christian endeavor has been left untouched. Various names have been attached to the phenomenon: charismatic renewal, neo-pentecostalism, classic Pentecostalism, the tongues movement. Yet, the most striking aspect of what is happening is typified in the premise on which this book is based. New Testament Christianity.

If there has to be a label, let it be that one.

New Testament Christianity is not new, it's merely being rediscovered. And, the fresh outpouring of God's Spirit that many believe is that promised in Joel 2: 28-32 and Acts 2: 17-21, has brought about in God's spiritual order the resurgence of the New Testament Church to an extent not known since the first century A.D.

But, what is the New Testament Church? How does it work? What is God saying to the Church? What is a local New Testament church like? This book endeavors to answer these and other questions, at least in part, by teaching and example. The chapters that follow are not a panacea for New Testament life but they give an insight not previously afforded in print.

That brash Episcopal priest was Dennis Bennett—his story is told in *Nine O'Clock in the Morning*—and he begins the body of this book by discussing the nature of the New Testament Church and its Biblical and historical basis. The second article, by Dan Malachuk, is on spiritual eldership, one of the most important foundation stones of New Testament Church life.

In the chapters immediately following, concrete examples of successful and thriving New Testament churches are set forth. The churches portrayed represent a cross section of similar assemblies throughout the world. They are not intended as ultimate examples of church operation, or as the most exemplary individual congregations in existence. The New Testament principle, in fact, necessitates a *moving on* in the Holy Spirit. If the representative churches have continued to follow the leading of that Spirit since these articles were written, they will have gone on to new heights and directions.

The geographic areas depicted are the Eastern, Southern, Midwestern, Northwestern, and Western United States; and England and Scotland. The basic criteria will apply almost anywhere in the world.

The final article in the book is by Dennis Baker and should be read and studied carefully. The article explains how those people experiencing the baptism by the Holy Spirit are drawn together into groups without regard for the usual religious and social boundaries.

Readers should bear in mind as they study this book that fulfillment of New Testament principles require three basic ingredients of belief and practice: Word, deed, signs and wonders. The kerygma, koinonia, and charisma. Or to put it another way: the Good News is to be preached, the brethren are to come together in fellowship, and the supernatural gifts of God are to be allowed to operate. (See Romans 15: 18-19)

That's the New Testament Church.

Al West

Authors

Dennis Baker is a graduate of Princeton Theological Seminary and is an editor in the Logos International book department. He is also an ordained Reformed Church minister and has served as a missionary in Mexico, a pastor in New Jersey, and as a charismatic teacher and speaker.

Dennis J. Bennett is pastor of St. Luke's Episcopal Church in Seattle, Washington, and in recent years has become one of the best known charismatic scholars and pastors in North America. He is author of *Nine O'Clock in the Morning* and coauthor, with his wife, Rita, of *The Holy Spirit and You.*

Jamie Buckingham is pastor of The Tabernacle Church in Melbourne, Florida, and is a graduate of Southwestern Baptist Theological Seminary. A well known Christian writer and author, his books include *Run Baby Run, Ben Israel, Some Gall,* and *Shout It From the Housetops.*

Michael Darwood is an English evangelist. He is editor of *Ripened Grain,* a publication of the *Good News Crusade,* has written various inspirational books and is coauthor of several Bible study publications.

John P. French is associate pastor of Calvary Church of the Valley, Scottsdale, Arizona, and is senior vice president of the Luce Press Clipping Service in Mesa, Arizona. He is a graduate of Washington and Lee University.

Father Joseph Fulton is the pastor of Blessed Sacrament Church in Seattle, Washington. He was a Dominican priest more than 30 years before he became personally involved in New Testament life. Since then, he says, his special ministry is "just letting things happen."

Jim Handyside is director of the Scottish Christian Witnessing Team (SCWT) at Clydebank, Scotland, near Glasgow. He has made a number of evangelistic trips to India, the United States, and Europe, and conducts an extremely active outreach ministry in his own country.

Jack W. Hayford is pastor of the First Four Square Church at Van Nuys, California. He is a graduate of Life Bible College and Azusa Pacific College.

Harry Lunn is a layman in a New Testament Church in Kansas City, Missouri. He has been active in charismatic endeavors for many years and has authored various articles and essays on New Testament life.

Daniel Malachuk is founder and president of Logos International, Inc., the Christian book publishers. Born and raised in New York City, he has been a spirit-filled Christian more than 35 years and is an elder in the First Christian Assembly, a New Testament church, Plainfield, N. J.

Joe Mallon has been active in the Catholic Pentecostal movement in Philadelphia, Pennsylvania, since its inception in 1968. He is employed by the Federal government and is a commentator in St. Martin's Church, Philadelphia.

Peter J. Marshall pastors the East Dennis Community Church on Cape Cod, in Massachusetts, and is a graduate of Princeton Theological Seminary. An outstanding minister in his own right, he is the son of the late Peter Marshall, former chaplain of the U. S. Senate, and famed writer, Catherine Marshall (Le Sourd); and stepson of Leonard Le Sourd, Editor of *Guideposts*.

Dick Schneider is Senior Editor of the famed Christian magazine, *Guideposts* and is an active Methodist layman. He lives in Morristown, N. J., and shepherds a New Testament prayer meeting.

Malcolm Smith has been pastor of Salem Gospel Tabernacle in Brooklyn, New York, since 1968 and is much sought after as a teacher and speaker. Formerly an evangelist and pastor in his native England, and in Ireland, he is author of the bestselling book, *Turn Your Back on the Problem.*

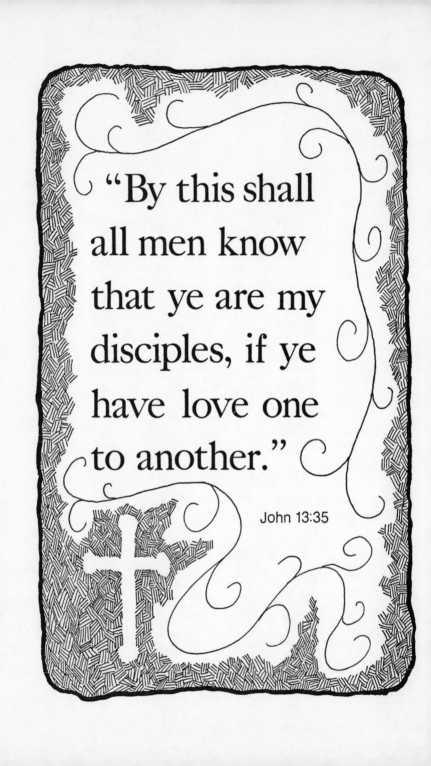

"By this shall all men know that ye are my disciples, if ye have love one to another."

John 13:35

What a New Testament Church Is

Dennis J. Bennett

The term "New Testament Church" has become a catch-phrase—part of the jargon of the day—but just what is a New Testament church? Some seem to think there is an unfulfilled pattern of the church set forth in the New Testament which is now being unfolded: God is doing a "new thing," they say. Certainly we can say that the church God is bringing into being today will be greater than the church in the New Testament —presumptuous though it may seem to say it—and in this sense will be fulfilling an unfulfilled pattern. But this does not mean that today we are to see a church that will be new in *essence*. Isaiah 43:19 is quoted: "Behold, I will do a new thing . . ." But in the context, you will see that God is saying to His people: "I am going to restore you, and the restoration will be so great and wonderful that you won't have to look back and hanker after what happened in days of old. This is going to be so much greater that you will hardly remember the former days, or bring to mind My earlier deliverances!" But that doesn't mean that God is doing something different in *nature* from what He has done before. God doesn't change; the "newness" is *renewal*—and renewal with a glory that we could not even imagine before we see it.

It seems to me important to begin any discussion of the "New Testament church," or the renewal of the fellowship of the people of God, with these observations, because if there is one thing that is weak among Christians who are involved in the charismatic or Pentecostal renewal today, it is a sense of history and continuity. If we lose our sense of history—that God has dealt with others in the past in the same basic way He is dealing with us—we are likely to get into real trouble. In fact, some groups already are so concerned with "restoration" that they are beginning to sit lightly toward the Scripture, which is, they say, after all, only a record of "former things."

God is renewing, correcting, reforming, empowering His people. One cannot blame Christians who have just been baptized in the Holy Spirit for thinking sometimes that because God is doing something new in their lives, He has therefore changed his ways with the church and the world. The breadth of new insight that opens to a believer when he or she is baptized in the Holy Spirit is so amazing and unexpected that it seems to be an entirely new and unsuspected world of spiritual experience, especially if that person has had little growth in personal experience of the Lord since conversion, or if, like Cornelius and his friends in Acts 10, the conversion and the Baptism in the Spirit follow one another in immediate succession. Yet it is not so. One of the very first things the Holy Spirit does is to point the believer back to the Scriptures and illuminate them, the inspired record of God's actions in the past. The Holy Spirit leads only to new things in the light of, and in communion and agreement with, the old.

In the Book of Revelation, the Lord exhorts the church at Ephesus to return to its *first* love, to do the *first* works. To the church at Sardis He says, "Strengthen the things that *remain*." Isaiah says, "In *returning* and rest shall ye be saved," and Jeremiah, "Ask for the *old* paths, where is the good way, and walk therein, and ye shall find rest for your souls." This divine conservatism is vitally important to us, lest we join the ranks of the unhappy "existential" moderns who maintain that the "only reality is change," and, if they believe in God, don't really know what He is like *now*, or where He is leading into an unknown future; or lest we be misled into an attempt to create a "New Testament" situation ourselves, which can lead all the way from the creation of little exclusivist groups like many that are springing up today, through the kind of violent enforcement of supposed "New Testament" principles that is seen, for example, in the "Children of God" movement and other aberrations that have troubled the "Jesus people" movement here and there, all the way to a full-scale scene of horror such as that the Anabaptists created at Munster in 1534, during the Reformation, through their insistence on the fulfilling of a supposed "New Testament" pattern in that city, which ended in a breakdown of everything including morality, and in the massacre of all the participants.

The New Testament church, therefore, is not something that is yet to come into existence; in a very real sense, it had always existed. It came into clear view in the time of the New Testament, and is now emerging again with even greater clarity. The "church," after all, means the blessed community of personal beings who are in fellowship with God. The word used in the New Testament that is translated "church" is *ekklesia,* which means a group of people who are called out—chosen. It is much stronger than "assembly," which could mean a group of people meeting together by their own consent and decision, while *ekklesia* implies people called out, called together by an authority or power beyond themselves, in this case, of course, by the Holy Spirit. Our word "church" in English, however, is derived from the Greek *kuriakos,* meaning "belonging to the Lord." If we take as the meaning of the "church" the blessed community and "called out" fellowship of those who belong to the Lord, and with the Lord, we begin to get the picture. The *Epistle to Diognetus,* one of the early writings of the period immediately following the New Testament, says of the church that she "existed in the very beginning, and for her sake the worlds were created".

It is not too farfetched to speak of the three Persons of the Godhead as constituting a "church," a blessed community, and this puts the idea of "church" right back into the very Essence of God himself. Indeed, this is exactly right, for while the highest forms of pagan (non-biblical) religion see the fulfillment of man as "*union* with God," loss of identity, dropping into nirvana, losing oneself in the "all," the Christian faith alone (fulfilling what was implicit in the faith of the Old Testament) sees the purpose of man's existence as *communion* or fellowship with God; not self-loss, but the heightening of personal identity to an infinite degree, in order that love and fellowship can be raised to infinity. (In Christianity, it is the "old man" that is destroyed, but the "new man" in Christ is to enjoy to the full his or her personal identity as the "friend of God" through Jesus Christ.) And in this, man is simply reflecting and sharing in the very Nature of God, for God not only desires community and fellowship—He is in Himself community and fellowship. God has never been alone! He never said, as James Weldon Johnson imagines him saying —in a beautiful but theologically misleading poem—"I'm lonely—I'll make me a

world!" God didn't need to create angels or me for company—or for community.

The tri-personal Godhead is in Himself a blessed community of Father, Son, and Holy Ghost. The experience of shared love and fellowship did not have to wait for the creation to be expressed and experienced, but was in the very Nature of God. When man fell from his original state, he lost fellowship with God, and thus the church was lost to man, until Jesus came to reestablish it on this earth. This reestablishment was actually begun in the Old Testament, when God chose Abraham, and then Israel—indeed in one place, Acts 7:38, Israel in the wilderness is called a "church"—but this was only looking toward the coming of the Savior who would really begin to build the church again on earth.

So the renewal of the church does not refer to government, order, methods, doctrines, teachings—important though these things may be in their place; rather, the renewal of the church must be the renewal of *fellowship*—first with God, and then, as a result, with man. The church, someone has said, is a "colony of heaven" on the earth. The nature of heaven is fellowship in complete love and acceptance, rejoicing in one another in the Lord. This is what the church *is,* and if it isn't this, it isn't the church.

Every church group has its ritual (form of words) and its ceremony (way of doing things); every group has its order and structure. It isn't the ritual, the ceremony, the order, or the structure that's of primary importance, though, but the *fellowship*. Without love and fellowship, any ceremony, whether it's the ceremony of raising one's hands to praise the Lord, or kneeling down to pray in a prayer meeting, is empty. Without love and fellowship, any ritual, whether it's the *Book of Common Prayer,* or an informal, "Praise the Lord! Hallelujah!" is empty. Without love and fellowship, any church order or structure will be a coldhearted thing, lifeless and dead.

The words, the actions, the order must arise out of a glowing of Jesus' love in the hearts of His people, or all we have is "formality," whether the church be Roman Catholic, Baptist, or Pentecostal.

Jesus' love shed abroad in our hearts is the true sign of the New Testament church. Jesus gave only one *new* commandment to his followers: "That you love one another as I have loved you." "By this," said He, "shall all men know that you are my disciples, by the

love that you have one for another" (John 13:34,35). It is the love of
Jesus that creates the church, and that holds the church in
fellowship. The apostle John says, with amazement, "We know that
we have passed from death into life because we love the brethren" (I
John 3:14).

"The kingdom of heaven is not meat and drink . . ." not even the
bread and wine of the Lord's Supper. Rightly offered, and rightly
received, the Holy Communion can indeed minister God's love and
fellowship, but not in and of itself—*ex opere operato*. The love of
Jesus must be there in the hearts of His people, ready to be stirred,
otherwise the most profound and meaningful acts of worship and
sacrament/ordinance are going to be purely external in their effect,
people seeking to draw near to God by works. The kingdom of God is
"righteousness, and peace, and joy in the Holy Ghost."
"Righteousness" means a right relationship with God through
Jesus Christ, and as a result, a right relationship with our fellow
creatures, in love and charity one with another. Thus we have
peace—and the whole moves in the joy of the Holy Ghost. This is the
true renewal, and then the sacraments/ordinances will be filled
with meaning and power, and church order will be a joy and a blessing.

Is it happening? Yes, it is—amazingly so. I have been a pastor
now for twenty-eight years, and I know that churches can
sometimes be centers of neurotic conflict between people. So
often—by no means always, thank God!—the people who emerge
into leadership in a church are those whose insecurity and drive for
recognition have brought them to the top. It is an old story that a
congregation can be torn apart by a feud between two people, or two
families. It is a truism that church leaders feel that "keeping the
peace" is the first requirement of "bishops and other ministers." I
have had it said to me more than once in one way or another by top
church administrators, when they have been discussing my
witness of the charismatic renewal, "Oh Dennis, we believe that the
church is in desperate need; we believe that what you are talking
about may be what is needed; but, oh, Dennis, we can't have any
trouble! Don't rock the boat! She's only barely afloat now!" Or, to
change the figure: "The old lady is dying, but she's dying quietly.
Please don't disturb her! One of the reasons God was unable to
work so freely at St. Luke's Episcopal Church back in 1960 was

that the boat had already sunk! We couldn't do it any harm!

With the acceptance of renewal through the Baptism or receiving of the Holy Spirit, all this changes, and changes overnight, if the people of the congregation will open their hearts to His work. When I came to St. Luke's, in Seattle, bringing my testimony of Jesus and the Baptism in the Holy Spirit (and I don't try to tell the whole story here, as it has been told in detail in the book *Nine O'Clock in the Morning*), the people were almost literally at each other's throats. The little church was torn with dissension. This ceased immediately. Why? Because even though it was several weeks before we actually got down to talking about the baptism in the Holy Spirit, the people of St. Luke's detected, I believe, that something had happened to me, and that my priorities were different, and this was in spite of the fact that I was really quite fearful about getting started witnessing to the work of the Holy Spirit in this new situation—I was looking for a period of peace and quiet. And as the leaders of the congregation began to receive the Baptism in the Holy Spirit, a new sense of the love of Jesus began to spread through the church.

People sometimes say to us at St. Luke's "Are you still using the *Prayer Book*? Are you still going through those Episcopalian services?" and the answer is "Yes, of course!" We may change these things somewhat—we have done so—as the years go by, and as the Spirit of God leads, but it wasn't a change of church order, or liturgy, that made the difference at St. Luke's, it was the "love of God shed abroad in our hearts," and to the extent that we experience that love and peace of Jesus in us, and among us, we *are* a New Testament church!

This love cannot be confined to *our* fellowship, or *our* group only, but must be extended to all our brothers and sisters who have received Christ. We can meet in small groups and fellowships, and I, for one, believe that the real flow of the love of God cannot take place in our midst until we are regularly meeting in small groups for fellowship in Jesus ("Where two or three are gathered . . ."—Jesus certainly believed in the believers meeting in small groups!), for the small group is protected by its fellowship in the love of the Lord, with other small groups, and all together in the unity of the whole Body of Christ. Here is the renewal of the church. The Holy Spirit is saying today, "Love one another! Love one another!" If we can stay in the fellowship of the Spirit, and in love one with another, then there is hope that our second- and third-level issues will be settled. If we can stay in fellowship in the Spirit and in the love of Jesus, then questions such as baptism, or interpretation of the Scripture, or methods of church government, will be settled by the Spirit and in the Spirit, and the New Testament church experience will be established right in the midst of our many denominations and groups, to draw us together into the only fellowship that matters: the fellowship of the Holy Spirit.

"This is a true saying, If a man desire the office of a bishop, he desireth a good work."

–I Tim. 3:1

Spiritual Eldership

Daniel Malachuk

Jesus said, "Wherever two or three are gathered in my name, I am in the midst."

Initially, the church was simple in form. The church never was an individual, but a corporate body of "members in particular." The holy universal church that is to be, when the Bridegroom has completed the process of lustration, having fully cleansed it by the "washing of water by the Word" (Eph. 5:26), is not the church as we see it with blemishes and imperfections. However, it is the *ideal* church for which we must strive, and I suggest that it should embody the following:

Faith — An experiential knowledge of Christ is imperative for each believer.

Fellowship — Each believer must be vitally joined to Christ, and all believers joined one to another in a living relationship.

Unity — Reconciling peoples and nations to God in His Spirit is the true ecumenical effort. Unity can be attained only through the baptism in the Holy Spirit.

Consecration — As Peter stated in I Peter 2:9, members of the church are an elect race, "a royal priesthood, an holy nation," a people of God's own possession.

Power — Power to witness and to function results from a personal Pentecost. Acts 1:8 reads, "But ye shall receive power, after that the Holy Ghost is come upon you; and ye shall be witnesses unto me both in Jerusalem, and in all Judaea, and in Samaria, and unto the uttermost part of the earth." This power is to last until the end of the world.

The organization of the church was by gradual growth and

emerging needs. Temple worship was adhered to, supplemented by apostolic teaching, prayer, fellowship, and breaking of bread. Two kinds of ministries became evident in Acts 6:2,4—prophetic and practical. The apostles fasted, studied, and prayed; the deacons waited on tables and ministered in temporal matters. In the sub-apostolic age the apostles became wandering evangelists of little standing, and the prophets became soothsayers. In Ephesians 2:20 Paul says Christians "are built upon the foundation of the apostles and prophets, Christ Jesus himself being the chief corner stone." The apostles were depositories of Christ's power, and the prophets held the mysteries of Christ. They were certainly needed then, and these ministries are certainly needed today. As prophetic inspiration to and in the church gradually died out in the first and second centuries, the bishops and deacons became prominent.

The Reformation of the sixteenth century was a protest and a return to scriptural principle and apostolic church order. The restoration of the ruling eldership was first suggested by Eculampadius, but John Calvin gave the thought life, form, and power. The church at Geneva included pastors, teachers, ruling elders, and deacons. Many early New England churches followed the Geneva pattern. In 1560 in Scotland, eldership was reinstated. Ministers were declared chief of the elders, in view of the fact that they were entrusted as pastors. Laymen ordained as ruling elders, however, were given equal authority with ministerial elders in all church courts.

In the Hebrew theocratic state, the elders were the legal representatives of the people and were organized into courts with lower and higher judications (Exod. 18:13-26). The highest of these courts was the council of seventy (Num. 11:16). During the time of Christ, the people associated in synagogues and congregations (Acts 13:15). In each congregation there was a chief ruler, and instruction was given by the legate or the doctor of the law. The elders were also in the bodies of the Sanhedrins; they exercised judicial functions within limited districts. The control of the religious state affairs was vested in a supreme council of priests, elders, and scribes. This was the great Sanhedrin. Under this Jewish system, our Lord lived. One of his first acts of ministry was performed in the synagogue of Nazareth (Luke 4:16), and the authority of the synagogue was recognized by him when he said, "tell it to the Church" (Matt. 18:17).

The primitive Christian church adopted some general features of the synagogues, modified in matters of detail by apostolic sanction. The officers who received the gifts which were sent to Jerusalem by the Antioch Christians were elders (Acts 11:30). Paul and Barnabas ordained elders (plural) in every church (Acts 14:23) regardless of size! It is indicated that elders were those entrusted to teach, rule, and preach.

Qualifications of an elder are stated in I Timothy 3:1-7; Titus 1:6-9; James 5:14; I Peter 5:1-4:
1. Exemplary piety, "blameless," of good behavior. An example to the believer.
2. Intelligence, "apt to teach," preach, and exhort.
3. Knowledge of the Truth.
4. Steadfastness in the faith.
5. Executive ability: "one that ruleth well his house."
6. Good reputation.
7. Judicial temperament: "One that ruleth well his own house, having his children in subjection with all gravity."
8. Not a recent convert (not a novice).
9. Capacity for prayer: "elders of the church, let them pray over him."
10. Sobriety, "sober," not given to wine.
11. Generosity, "not covetous," given to hospitality.
12. Temperance and prudence (not self-willed, temperate).
13. Gravity and lover of justice.
14. Patience and gentleness: "no striker," "not soon angry."
15. Carefulness as to his associates: "a lover of good men."
16. Energy and watchfulness—vigilant and full of the Holy Spirit with a fruitful ministry.

Inasmuch as an elder is divinely appointed, it is apparent to the ministers and church members that he has been ordained of God to rule as an elder. The individual also knows his calling. The church today needs laymen to share in the spiritual ministry of the church and to promote the message of Christ, if we are to present the Christian Gospel to all the world. Not too long ago, a statement was made that arrested my attention. It was in the form of a question: "Where are the spiritual elders of the church?" They were not referring to the officeholders but to men of spiritual stature fulfilling the scriptural qualifications of elders.

I am reminded lately of the many conferences I have had with ministers, and as they unburden their hearts, they too sense a need for spiritual elders to fulfill duties in the administration and spiritual programs of their churches. When polls indicated that over 60 percent of the ministers claim administration is taking too much time, and almost 50 percent are finding too little time left for study and prayer, I began to look for some answers to an old problem. One writer suggested the church consider hiring professional business managers for administration purposes. In my own personal discussions with ministers of various denominations, I have heard that the lack in their churches was spiritual eldership. Ordinarily, we depend upon one man to solve the spiritual problems of the church, but we need men who have had a personal experience, as recorded in John 3:5-8.

"Jesus answered, Verily, verily, I say unto thee, Except a man be born of water and of the Spirit, he cannot enter into the kingdom of God."

"That which is born of the flesh is flesh; and that which is born of the Spirit is spirit."

"Marvel not that I said unto them, Ye must be born again."

"The wind bloweth where it listeth, and thou hearest the sound thereof, but canst not tell whence it cometh, and whither it goeth: so is every one that is born of the Spirit."

This is the doorway to power and to the nine gifts of the Holy Spirit (I Cor. 12:7-11). The experience of the early Christians is available today for those men desiring to be spiritual elders (Acts 1:4-5; 2:4).

God has not changed, and neither has the need for spiritual elders to co-labor with the pastor. The pastor, who is an elder, needs other elders to assist him in overseeing the spiritual development of the congregation, and knowing the pulsebeat of the members. In both the Old and New Testaments, elders were prominently featured and recognized. In the charismatic ministry, the elder, like the prophet or messenger of God, is coexistent with the church. An Elder who is not God-ordained, however, is a hindrance rather than a blessing. Serious consideration should be given by church members and pastors to the valued ministry of spiritual elders in the light of the scriptures. Bible study of an elder's ministry and his qualifications should be undertaken. Elders should not be appointed or elected on the basis of a popularity contest, but by the scriptural standard. The present day charismatic revival is producing an excellent caliber of Christian laymen, and many of these men can fulfill the scriptural qualifications of an elder. A man who has experienced the baptism in the Holy Spirit has a sincere desire to perform services to his church. One of the results of the baptism in the Holy Spirit is a desire to witness to the Lord Jesus Christ, and to serve the church in a greater measure. A spiritual man seeks spiritual expression.

It is proper for men to desire the office of an elder, if such office is established (1 Tim. 3:1):

"This is a true saying, If a man desire (aspire RSV) the office of a bishop, he desireth a good work."

Opportunity for spiritual men should be provided in the church. If it is not, the individual will seek some agency which will offer him the expression he needs. I believe the failure of the church to provide expression for laymen has resulted in the fraternal and secular men's organizations which we have today, many of which are but substitutes for the programs and purposes which the church should have provided.

God has not changed—elders were given to the church to assist in the spiritual government of the church. How can congregations "call for the elders of the church" (James 5:14) if there are no recognized elders in the congregation? Many of the larger traditional churches are encouraging a greater spiritual lay activity. It is impossible for the church, with its present number of clergymen, to minister to the needs of the world. Dr. Joseph G. Moore, in *The Living Church* stated: "We can never afford to have enough clergy unless 90 percent are men who give their time to the church and earn their living as lawyers, engineers, carpenters, etc."

Elders participating in worship services will make services more interesting. The Holy Spirit works through more than one individual, and as more individuals are used the congregation will become inspired. The greater the participation of members, the greater the growth for individuals and for the corporate whole. Churches involved in inner-city programs can profit by the examples of "mother" churches by establishing "storefront" and city missions of 100 to 150 people and appointing their elders in charge of these works. Many inner-city churches, contemplating closing their doors because of membership shifts, can profit from these experiments and fulfill the admonition of the Lord in "going out and making disciples."

As laymen and church leaders are becoming awakened through the present charismatic revival, churches must examine traditions, search the scriptures, and set their houses in order. I can see consistent revival and church expansion only as we become obedient to God's Word. This is the hour of the drawing together of God's hosts: "Like a mighty army moves the church of God, Brothers we are treading where the saints have trod."

BY HIS SPIRIT

A Modern-Day New Testament Church

Dick Schneider

Every Sunday morning an investment counselor in New Jersey takes part in the 8:00 a.m. Holy Communion at his Episcopal church, then drives thirty miles to Plainfield, where he steps into the First Christian Assembly, sits down on a plain varnished pew, and raises his arms in praise of the Lord.

Join him and the 250 others who pack this New Testament church and you'll get an idea of what attracts worshipers from fourteen different Protestant denominations, plus a sizable group of Catholic Pentecostals.

The Holy Spirit is here. He moves unhindered through the congregation like the wind through a wheat field. You see Him in the tears of joy streaming unashamed down their cheeks, in the peace of those quietly savoring His comfort.

You hear Him in the spontaneous singing of Psalms, in the joyful handclapping.

And you know Him in the prophecy which rings out from the elders and in the words of the pastor who speaks in the Spirit.

It seems all the more miraculous when you learn that five years ago this was a staid little church dutifully following a traditional service format and not really going anywhere.

What happened?

"In a sense, the First Christian Assembly experienced a Baptism in the Holy Spirit," according to one of its three elders (the pastor and elders hold the equivalent of equal status). "Just as it sometimes takes a number of years for a person to become one with the Lord, it took our church seventeen years to really become a Body of Christ," he said.

"We started out as a group of searching Christians which met in members' homes. As we grew in number, we rented space from a church, then met in a former art gallery, and finally moved into our own building.   "But," adds another elder, "we more or less groped our way along as a small Pentecostal church."

"The change came in 1969," points out the third elder, "when, instead of trying to run the church ourselves, we turned it over to the Lord.

"His holy inspiration came, and the First Christian Assembly has never been the same since. One of the first signs of the moving of the Lord came when He brought the present pastor, David Hannon, to the church in 1969."

David Hannon had already gone through his own experience.

"When I was twenty," he says, "I had a milk-truck route and practically no interest in the deeper life, beyond going through the motions of Sunday church attendance.

"One day our truck mechanic asked me 'Are you a professing or a possessing Christian?'

"He invited me to an evangelistic meeting at his church, and it was there I met the Lord. However, my life went along pretty much the same as it was. I was quite active playing semipro baseball, and at one of the games a young man witnessed to me.

'But I've given my life to Christ,' I said.

'Yes,' he answered, 'but have you had the Baptism in the Holy Spirit?'

"I was intrigued and began attending his Swedish Pentecostal church, and that's where it happened."

On fire with the Lord, Hannon went to Northeast Bible Institute, then pastored various churches, joined the faculty of Elim Bible Institute's branch in Brooklyn, gained his B. A. degree from Central Bible College in Springfield, Missouri, and worked closely with Ben Crandall, pastor of Calvary Tabernacle in Brooklyn.

It was in Brooklyn that Bob Mumford referred him to the Plainfield church.

Leaders of the church decided that the choice of a new pastor should rest with the congregation. So for one month David Hannon preached on Sunday mornings and evenings and taught at Wednesday evening services. By the end of the month he became pastor by a unanimous decision.

"It was at this time that we really became a church with a multiple ministry," says Pastor Hannon.

"There is no single leader at First Christian Assembly," he explains. "According to the Scriptures, every church that Paul established was administered by elders. He never placed one man in authority. Thus, all major decisions were made by the elders together in prayer. We were led by the Holy Spirit to do the same at First Christian Assembly."

It has worked out well. Under the three elders and the pastor, a continuity of leadership is assured. If Pastor Hannon is out of town, one of the elders takes over.

"Even when I'm present," says David Hannon, "we sometimes receive guidance that an elder is to lead the service." The other elders are George Herman, Richard Malachuk, and Dan Malachuk.

This complete trust in the Holy Spirit governs every church activity. And since the order of worship is left up to Him, Sunday mornings are never exactly the same from one week to the next.

It results in an exciting spontaneity.

Morning worship begins at 10:45 with a happy, expectant congregation breaking out in song. There are no printed programs, though one of the elders will usually lead the singing. And even though hymnals are available for new people, it's interesting to see how quickly they put the books down to join in singing from the heart.

Sometime during the service, the pastor or elder will give a message, an invitation will be offered for those who wish to come forward for the ministry of laying on of hands, prophecies resound, and testimonies are given by members of the congregation. So that these testimonies may be heard easily, microphones drop down from the ceiling at strategic intervals among the pews.

One of the most inspiring sights during the service is when worshipers stand to greet one another as brothers and sisters in Christ with joyful handshakes and embraces. This at-oneness between people of different races and denominations is a preview of what it will be like when Christ returns.

Morning services end around 12:30 p.m. though they may close later, depending on the Spirit. The Spirit is also allowed to move through the church school which precedes the services. First Christian Assembly people feel there is no point in withholding the good news of the Baptism from children. Moreover, the youngsters are encouraged to praise the Lord openly. When they take part in worship services, they find it perfectly natural and enjoyable to praise Him fully, with no thought of hanging back in embarrassment.

You'll find a goodly number of children at the Sunday evening and Wednesday evening services, too. Wednesday evening usually brings outside speakers; many of these have been Catholic Pentecostals, such as Father Joseph Orsini from Bayonne, New Jersey.

Spontaneity extends to offerings, too, not only in the method, in which sometimes the congregation will march to music past the collection plate, but in the spirit of giving.

No one "pledges" at First Christian Assembly.

"We feel that when one signs a pledge, he limits himself on what he will do," states Herman. "We believe that the amount of one's gift should be governed only by the inspiration of the Holy Spirit at the time it is made."

As a result, there is no financial problem at First Christian Assembly. In fact, the church helps support a dozen missionaries throughout the world. It has also purchased a nearby apartment building to be used as a center in helping prepare laymen for ministering elsewhere.

"We feel the Lord is calling us to develop leaders to help build the Body of Christ in other areas," says Pastor Hannon.

Already, First Christian Assembly is supplying teachers for home prayer groups, some as far as forty miles away. This expanding outreach can be seen in the church's own youth program, highlighted by regular Friday-night meetings, now attended by some forty youths.

The concept developed into an unusual church-sponsored trip in which nineteen youths, each paying his own way, traveled with Pastor Hannon to Surinam, South America, in the Fall of 1971, where they worked with evangelist Claire Hutchins. For one week the young people witnessed in street meetings, sang in evening crusade services, and assisted in teens' and children's meetings. Accompanying the group from the United States were two Roman Catholic priests and nuns, and they provided entry into Surinam Catholic churches where Pastor Hannon spoke on the baptism in the Holy Spirit.

What will happen next at First Christian Assembly?

"Only Jesus knows," says Pastor Hannon. "And that's the exciting part of it. Our endeavor is to remain flexible to His moving. We can't allow past policies and tradition to dictate.

"We have learned that even as Pentecostals, we can have as many hang-ups in this respect as other denominations which adhere to rigid forms. For it is human nature to resist change.

"But when we turn our church over to Him, these human fetters fall away, and He gives us the grace to move along with Him. And when the Spirit moves unhindered, miracles happen."

For the past several years at First Christian Assembly, it has been one continuous miracle.

An Inner City New Testament Church

Malcolm Smith

I gave up trying to produce a New Testament church more than two years ago. Shattered with total defeat in every area of life and ministry, I handed what was left over to the Holy Spirit.

My first sight of Salem Gospel Tabernacle was not the most inspiring. The church stood forlornly on the windswept corner of 4th Ave. and 54th St. in Brooklyn. Trash filled the gutters and beer cans were crushed into the potholed street outside. A newspaper was wrapped around the church railings, held there by a chill wind that was blowing. The B.M.T. Subway roared beneath the pavement on its way to Manhattan and Queens.

The bleak outside was suggestive of the spiritual condition inside. The congregation had been in revival some 45 years before but, as the years rolled by, the pews became emptier, a mocking reminder of better days. The area had contributed to this condition as the tree-lined avenue had become a low rent housing area and increasingly dangerous to walk at night.

My first sight of this was the early spring one year during a mission I was called to conduct. We came to pastor in the summer of the same year. I had been in the ministry for many years, but facing the challenge of the emptying church and the crying needs of Brooklyn, I realized that *although I was a minister I did not know how to minister.*

Outwardly the church had everything in order. It could boast of purity in doctrine, crossing all its evangelical t's and dotting all its i's. No one was allowed into membership without a clear testimony to being born again, and we spelled out our belief in our bylaws that every Spirit-filled Christian should speak in tongues. Our view of the church was as close to the New Testament as we could make it and boasted of being a local sovereign assembly who received their direction from God and not from a manmade H.Q. We had a board of elders who took the spiritual leadership in the congregation. Like the Pharisees, everything we believed was right—*dead right.*

No one was joining our pure membership, only leaving or dying, for no one was being born again though we had an evangelistic service every Sunday night with the best program that we knew how to have. Although we insisted on the baptism in the Holy Spirit being defined as "with speaking in other tongues," very few did and no one was receiving the experience. It was very wonderful to state that the church was governed by God but, as a congregation, we did not know how to receive the leading of the Spirit. As the pastor over this pathetic situation I was probably worse than any for I did not know how to enter a flow of the Spirit myself, and had thrashed furiously for two years trying to make that beautiful New Testament church pattern work, and had failed totally.

We had to learn that there is no pattern in the New Testament that can be imitated. The history and letters of the New Testament are rather the description of the spontaneous result of the Holy Spirit working through a group of believers in a local situation. It is not a pattern that we go to, to see how they did this or that, and then to slavishly copy it, but rather a challenge that, as we will yield to the same Spirit, will accomplish the same results. Not us copying the model but rather the architect Himself, from *within that company of people,* building His church in every location and in every generation.

And so, finally I stopped trying to build His Church, stopped trying to fit together the stones, and handed it all over to Him. At once the church was plunged into a revival that we are only recently beginning to fully realize.

At the onset, we knew nothing of what He was doing. In fact, everything seemed to be the same. It is only in retrospect that we realize the enormous change that has taken place in every facet of our lives.

It was a subtle change because we did not exactly learn anything brand new. We had believed the right things for years but had forgotten what they meant. The Holy Spirit began to light them up to us and excite us with them, weaving them into the very life of the church. The first thing that happened was we began to discover who we were. We found that we could never *go to church because we were the church*. The church is not a building of bricks and mortar, but of people who are alive with the life of Jesus. Peter calls them "living stones" and he says we are built into the Foundation Stone, Jesus Christ. In this temple of God, expressed locally in a company of believers, the Holy Spirit lives and expresses the ascended Jesus. We had been guilty of speaking of Jesus alive in the twentieth century as if He was someone who walked down the aisle of the church. An Invisible Evangelist who walked by and touched people. Now we saw that His being alive was in His Body, the church, and He lived in Brooklyn, in the company of believers. He still spoke and worked His miracles, but did so through His Body, the stones being made alive with His life. It was a heady experience as the church became tinglingly aware that when they met, the Body of Christ was come together. Jesus was in the midst, not as the Person filling an extra pew, but there in each, and in all and through all.

Along with this came the immediate comprehension of our ministry. The stones are also the priests. Not only do they make the Temple, but they are the ministers of the Temple. We had spoken for years about the priesthood of every believer, but now we came gradually alive to the fact that we had one ministry only, a priestly ministry to God. We had tried to have a ministry in every direction, to every kind of person and strata of society, but all had failed because we did not have the ministry of the priest Godward. With this understanding, our gathering together became different. Our services had been the Evangelical Club Sandwich variety. A variety of hymns, interspersed with choir, special music, announcements, and a very occasional testimony. A spontaneity began to happen that stole upon us in such a way that no one could really say exactly when it happened. Worship began to rise from the heart of the gathered congregation, worship that was spontaneous and uninhibited. People began to raise their hands, sing praises to God, and even clap their hands for the sheer wonder of the God they adored. We might not get started on the first hymn until 20 minutes after the service had begun because of the flow of worship that began as the meeting opened. Hymns were sung as a necessary expression of the joy and praise within, *now,* instead of something done in church on a Sunday. The gifts of the Spirit, that had been in the church, became an integral part of the services and the life of the church during the week.

At first, I was wondering if we had seen the last of visitors. I was sure that they would be offended by the noise and lack of announced direction in the meetings. Instead, the reverse was true. People from all walks of life came, drawn by Unseen Hands, and drank in the Presence of God·that was increasingly being felt. Everyone relaxed in our priestly office and let Him build His church, one that was becoming New Testament-like without our trying to make it so.

And build it He did and is continuing to do so. In the beginning of the awakening of the church to worship, He plunged us into evangelism beyond all our wildest tryings of past years. A phone call from one of our members asking that we come speak to her neighbors about Christ started our home Bible meetings. We found that Brooklyn was full of people who were tired of organized religion, tired of sin and rebellion and wanting to receive the message of Jesus Christ. They came into homes and eagerly received the message and testimonies of excited Christians sharing their faith. The home meetings never became an end in themselves, but were under the direction of the elders, and became the hand of the church reaching out to the lost sheep in the concrete jungle. We have never used the meetings to advertise the church. The Holy Spirit made it very clear that He would bring those into the congregation who were to come. Gradually the people finding Christ in the homes found their way to the meetings of the church and became a vital part of the congregation.

One day we realized He had brought about a very beautiful situation. The church of living stones gathered at the weekend for teaching and worship. The Friday night Bible study, the Sunday services, all were for the teaching of the saints and for worshipping together, ministering one to another ... the Body of Christ gathered. Then during the week we became the Body scattered throughout New York City; lights that shone in the darkness, reaching out into the darkness and bringing others to Christ. We would come back at the weekend to introduce the new believers who had been harvested during the week, and to teach and send them forth.

I remember dreaming idealistically in former days of this and saying it was the way the early church operated. Yet I could never make it work then, the people never saw it that way. Now the Holy

Spirit made it happen and no one can quite pin down when and how it occurred.

The face of the congregation began to change, from the original Scandinavian immigrants who started the church, to an "all nations" kind of audience. And not only all nations, but all cultures, including hippies and kids from the drug scene. When they first walked in, I wondered how the congregation would receive them. They filed into the pews with their long hair, blue jeans and sweat shirts. I whispered, "Lord, will the congregation receive them?" At once the Spirit told me, "Of course, I wouldn't have sent them unless you were ready for them." So it was! The congregation received them with love and open arms.

As we looked to the future we knew that many ministries were there in the Body. Some of these began to emerge, others we sensed were undeveloped and awaiting encouragement. Some kind of training was needed to develop what had been given by the Spirit. We waited and listened for the Master Builder's next move. It came when one of the new converts asked if I could give him a listing of Bible schools since he felt a need for further training with a view to some ministry. I knew then we were being lead to a Bible training program, but we did not act at once. We waited until a dozen others from the congregation asked for a school. Finally, with the Holy Spirit nudging within and the newly converted asking from without, we opened a school in the basement of the church building. Each morning of the week, the students gather to learn of the Word of God, spend time in worship, and to be taught by waiting upon God. It is not a school recognized by major denominations, nor are any degrees given. We are not against such schools, but we feel He has laid it upon us to train our own congregation in the ministry He has given, and to send forth those trained to fulfill that ministry. The flow of ministry will itself be the "degree."

At a recent gathering of the Body of believers we shared together the great things God has done. One after another jumped to his or her feet to share or testify. I remembered the days when one antique testimony would have to be dragged out of the meeting but, now, they were spontaneous, bringing a flow of life. I looked over the rows of teenagers and those in their early twenties, so many of them delivered from the drug scene; from meaningless, purposeless existence, now saved and filled with the Holy Spirit. That night, as a congregation, we humbly acknowledged that no one person was responsible for what we saw and heard—it was a work of the Holy Spirit in which we had been involved by the grace of God.

Is it a perfect church, then? No, no more than the churches in the New Testament. We are very conscious of being in a learning situation, and very aware that there is so much He has yet to teach us. All we know is that He took a traditional Pentecostal assembly and caused us to remember why we were saved; to minister unto the Lord, and be the local expression of the Body of Christ.

He
must
increase,
but

I
must
decrease.

A Midwestern New Testament Church

Harry Lunn

During the last ten years, I have attended Evangelistic Center Church at 1024 Truman Road in Kansas City, Missouri, on a fairly regular basis. Unquestionably, it is an extraordinary church, a unique church. It is a charismatic church with a free flow of supernatural tongues and interpretations, prophetic utterance, and songs in the Spirit. There is liberty without license, freedom without disorder.

During the last eighteen years, hundreds and probably thousands have found Christ as their Savior, Lord, Baptizer, and Healer at the Center. We let the Lord keep the records.

Ten years ago, during a time of great personal stress, I discovered Evangelistic Center. As I began to move in the church, it soon became for me "a hiding place from the wind, and a cover from the tempest; like rivers of water in a dry place, like the shadow of a great rock in a weary land" (Isa. 32:2).

There is life at the Center. Its reputation is worldwide. When charismatic personalities from other areas and other countries visit Kansas City, they frequently come to the Center for rest and renewal. Our hospitality is boundless. Many well-known charismatics have spoken from the pulpit at the Center, some of them several times.

Rev. A.J. Rowden, the only pastor the Center has had, was ordained in the Evangelical United Brethren denomination more than thirty years ago. Although pastor of a thriving, prosperous EUB church in Louisiana, and in good standing with his denomination, Rev. Rowden was dissatisfied. It was always embarrassing for him to read the New Testament, then to compare his ministry with that of the New Testament preachers.

Apostolic power was lacking in his ministry, and he knew it. As he and his beloved wife, Margaret, went to God in prayer in a petition for spiritual power, the conviction merely deepened—and the dissatisfaction increased steadily.

Finally the Lord brought him into contact with a Pentecostal evangelist by the name of Everett Parrott, who spelled out the baptism in the Holy Spirit as the source of spiritual power. Convinced and fully persuaded, Pastor Rowden sought the experience. Both he and Margaret were baptized in the Spirit in a short while. Launching into a Full Gospel ministry almost immediately, they tried to introduce their congregation to the experience.

The reaction and consequences can be predicted. This occurred in the mid-forties, long before charismatic renewal reached the historic denominations in anything approaching its current intensity. In a short while, Pastor Rowden lost his church and was expelled from his denomination.

The epilogue can be found in a news release which appeared in charismatic publications several years ago. The release stated that in California all Evangelical United Brethren pastors, with two exceptions, had been baptized in the Holy Spirit with the initial evidence of glossolalia. The Lord knows how to vindicate His own.

Led by the Spirit each step of the way, Rev. Rowden pastored several interdenominational charismatic churches, with congregations made up mostly of believers who had suffered experiences similar to that of their pastor and his wife—ejection from their denominations after being baptized in the Holy Spirit.

As A.J. and Margaret sought the Lord earnestly in prayer, they experienced an increasingly compelling urge to come to Kansas City, and finally yielded to what was much more than an impulse. It was the Lord leading them, and they knew it.

Literally depending on the Lord for their daily bread, with nothing to sustain them but their faith in Him—which He confirmed daily—the Rowdens obtained a small building on Linwood Boulevard and began to minister the things of the Spirit to a small congregation, which became steadily larger.

Soon they moved to a larger building at Thirty-Fourth and Michigan, and continued to prosper. While traveling on a California freeway in 1962, Pastor Rowden received a revelation from the Lord of a new location which He had prepared for the

Center in Kansas City; He let him know that it was located near the confluence of centrally located freeways.

Returning to Kansas City, Pastor Rowden found the building almost immediately. It proved to be a fine edifice, formerly housing the Friendship Baptist Church, located at 1024 Truman Road. It was strategically located near the confluence of two major freeways. It was a beautiful brick building, wonderfully constructed, with all the needed facilities except adequate parking space, which was eventually provided through the acquisition of an adjacent property.

Contacting the owner, Pastor Rowden soon negotiated the acquisition of the property, and sold the property at Thirty-Fourth and Michigan for nearly as much as the cost of the new location. It was an unbelievable transaction, all arranged and provided by the Lord—who took care of everything.

In the first paragraph, we used the word "unique" in describing the church—which is no exaggeration. A church even approximating the Center in some of its characteristics will not be found anywhere. This does not indicate that the church is in error. It merely means that when His Spirit is allowed to exercise control, the Lord is willing to allow congregations as well as individuals to develop according to the needs of the community in which the church is located. When allowed to do so, the Lord delights in decorating a congregation with spiritual graces, in much the same way that He decorates a landscape with natural beauty. Stereotyping is man's idea, not the Lord's.

Perhaps the Lord's reason for allowing the Center to develop uniquely is to be found in its impact upon the community. Over the years, no church has been more influential in generating charismatic renewal in the Kansas City metropolitan area than Evangelistic Center. This can be verified in dozens of instances. With Kansas City rapidly becoming a focal point for the entire Jesus Movement, the Center has been a vital and positive factor in tipping the balance in favor of renewal.

When one examines the spirituality of the Center, he sees that the Lord's wisdom and purpose in the church is fully manifested. Although the Rowdens paid a high price for their courage in the early years of their charismatic ministry, both they and the congregation are reaping rich rewards now. For it is here at the

Center that one finds the full flowering of the Lord's purpose in the church. It can all be summed up in one word: worship.

Many Pentecostals and charismatics are under the impression that the ultimate purpose of the Pentecostal experience is to be found in the acquisition of spiritual power for witnessing and evangelization. This is an important facet of the experience, but it is not the supreme purpose by any means. The ultimate purpose is found in John's Gospel, chapter 4, verses 23,24:

"But the hour cometh, and now is, when the true worshippers shall worship the Father in spirit and in truth; for the Father seeketh such to worship him. God is a Spirit: and they that worship him must worship him in spirit and in truth."

Let me try to describe worship at Evangelistic Center. Informality and spontaneity are in evidence. The entire atmosphere is relaxed. There is seldom any need to try to generate spirituality, since it usually flows naturally. This is a mature congregation with none of the hang-ups which generate fear, apprehension, and tension among those who have had little experience in charismatic spirituality.

Sometimes a printed program is provided, which consists mostly of announcements concerning needs and forthcoming activities within the congregation. The worship service is never programmed, for no one knows what will happen—and the Lord seldom tells us in advance.

Usually the service starts with a few songs and choruses, followed by pastoral announcements, introduction of visitors, a few testimonies—frequently unsolicited, but usually purposeful—eventually an unpressurized offering, and finally, the pastor's sermon.

At some point during the service described above, the Holy Spirit usually takes over for an interim, and no one knows exactly when or where it will happen. The anticipation adds much to the quality of what occurs, for we know it will be spontaneous—the work of the Lord and His Spirit, not man.

Quite often it will start with a song in the Spirit, sometimes in English, sometimes in a supernatural tongue—followed by the interpretation. It is not unusual for one singer to bring forth the song in a tongue, then for another to sing the interpretation. Some of the voices are operatic in quality—developed by the Lord, not by man, for most of the singers have had no formal training whatever.

Frequently there are other supernatural utterances. Some take the form of direct prophecy. Others are brought forth in tongues, followed by interpretations. The miracle here is to be found in the fact that the supernatural utterances in song, prophecy, and interpreted tongues are invariably closely related and in harmony with each other. These utterances are blended like the elements of a symphony. Verbal nuances are expressed in which everyone finds something which applies to him. Only the Lord could do this, for it is all unplanned. One finds evidence of this in the Center's bimonthly publication, *Gospel,* which is distributed to the ends of the earth—including every state in the union.

Another miraculous facet is to be found in the blending of the supernatural utterances with the sermon which follows. The pastor's sermons are practically never announced in advance. Seldom is anyone aware of the sermon topic. Nonetheless, the prophetic utterances frequently blend perfectly with the sermon. This would indicate that the same Lord has authorized both the prophetic utterances and the sermon.

What is the purpose behind these supernatural utterances? Once again, it can all be summed up in one word: worship. These utterances invariably fall within the purview of I Cor. 14:3, and they always trigger worship. As the congregation is encouraged by these utterances, the believers lift their hands in submission and surrender as they praise and worship Jesus. Sometimes there is wave after wave of worship. It may last but a few moments; it has been known to continue for more than an hour.

One finds in all this none of the exhibitionism sometimes associated with the early Pentecostals. Although the worship is always orderly and in good taste, the uninitiated frequently find it objectionable because it offends their carnal sensibilities. The carnal mind does not lend itself to the worship of Jesus.

That which has made possible the kind of worship described above is to be found in the complete restoration of the gifts of the Spirit enumerated in I Cor. 12:8-10, the Body ministry described in the rest of the chapter, and the ministry gifts defined in Eph. 4:11,12.

Observers have repeatedly described Evangelistic Center as God's armory, in which the army of the Lord is equipped and trained in the use of spiritual weapons needed to conduct successfully a spiritual warfare. Actually, the Center combines the functions of a church, spiritual armory, and Bible school. Through the years, hundreds of workers, pastors, and evangelists have been trained, equipped, and sent forth by the Lord from the Center. Their exploits have become legendary as they have circled the earth.

The factor which has frequently made other pastors popeyed with amazement is the financing of the Center. The congregation has no fixed membership. New members are not inducted into the Center as in other churches. There is actually a floating membership, some permanent and some temporary, which fluctuates between 500 and 1,000. The church supports the pastors, A.J. and Margaret, one or more assistant pastors, three radio programs, three missionary families in Latin America, *Gospel* magazine, Charisma Bible School, and two annual pastoral conventions in May and October (they are enormously expensive). Gifted with an apostolic ministry, Pastor Rowden is a world traveler, and he has been responsible for establishing and ministering to many churches here and abroad—additional expense.

In spite of the tremendous expense incurred in keeping these activities current and solvent, all financing is low-keyed. There are no frantic appeals for money, no begging, no fund-raising programs in the traditional sense. Only once have I witnessed any anxiety in financing the church's programs—the purchase of the property needed to expand parking facilities—and it was finally resolved successfully.

Where does all the money come from? Most of the congregation tithe their income, some give much more than a tithe, and the Lord supplies the rest—much of it from anonymous donors.

What shall we say of the Center? How shall we describe the quintessence of its spirituality? Simply by this: If the Center were the only church in the world, it would immediately set out to evangelize the world. It is a New Testament church.

A West Coast New Testament Church

Jack W. Hayford

That first evening there were eighteen people sitting in an auditorium designed for over two hundred. The Lord's words to me many weeks before, "You're going to pastor a small church," were more precisely fulfilled than I would have guessed; I would have expected at least fifty.

But it was the Lord who had brought us to this moment, and it must be confessed that no great demonstration of faith was required to take the step of accepting this tiny pastorate. My position as dean of students at our denomination's largest college secured my status economically and ecclesiastically, and as I spoke to the small group of saints (the average age over sixty years) there was no personal risk involved. But little did I know that before long, God would require me to resign the security of position, prestige in man's eyes, and would summon me toward the prospect of obscurity.

A review of that first meeting, with a forthright confession of my own tendency to see things then as man would see them, is essential to reporting with clarity what has occurred at "The Church on the Way," the Van Nuys, California, Foursquare Church. The essence of what produced a congregation of several hundreds in such a short time lies in the Holy Spirit's bursting the plaster casts of tradition. We believe He is teaching us the divine therapy for any church crippled by ecclesiasticism. It discards crutches, and the legs being stripped of the casts' rigidity can be rubbed down with the oil of anointing and the body restored to mobility.

That our congregation was of the historic Pentecostal tradition is illustrative of the point that the Spirit of God can rise beyond the limits of a local church's history. One may think old-line denominational churches harder to awaken, but I know hundred of brethren in traditionally Pentecostal churches who will attest to the contrary.

Every generation needs its own revival, and the second and third generation inheriting a revival-founded denomination faces a greater challenge than those who find themselves surrounded by stained-glass sterility in a movement twice-dead. Resurrection is clearly required and easily the discernible need. But there is a temptation to suppose the patient in better health than is truly the case, to nurse and pamper the breathing body rather than commanding it to rise in the Name of Jesus and walk in the strength of her youth.

And so the Lord Jesus graciously began with a gentle hand. He led us—my wife Anna, the four children and myself—to the San Fernando Valley, and began to teach a small congregation the simplicity and joy of New Testament life. The personal aspects of the process by which bondage to human modes of thought was broken are important but won't be detailed here since this report is a summary of some of the basic principles contributing to the manifest blessing of God in this little church.

It is completely coherent to the pattern that things have taken to outline these principles with introductory remarks quoting men from our fellowship. In inviting comment from our eight-man council as I wrote these words, I emphasized the fact that there is participation of the members of the body of the congregation in everything we do. During that first service, mentioned at the beginning of the article, II Corinthians 4:1-7 provided the text for the brief message that followed our introduction as new pastor. The "we" of verses 1 and 7 involves the total congregation, a local body of believers—a mere clay vessel—in which God invests the fullness of the person of Jesus. From that time, we underscored the fact that my God-given calling as pastor was not one which made me "the minister." Rather, "pastor" was my place of ministry in the local body. The challenge to the believers was to grow in the discovery of their ministries coupled with my responsibility as pastor to so feed and lead them that their growth and development would contribute to and nourish that discovery. As a result, we have become a Christ-exalting, "ministry centered" people.

God has given me like-minded co-laborers in Chuck Shoemake and Paul Charter, who are used with their families in the significant area of teaching and youth ministry. Paul and his wife, Jerri, lead an every-Friday youth meeting which combines the best features of coffeehouse, Jesus-music festivals, and evangelistic preaching to result in weekly decisions for Christ and kids baptized in the Holy Spirit. Chuck's sensitivity to people and effective communication of practical spiritual truth especially complements the preaching-teaching ministry God has granted me; and his wife, Ruby, ministers with unusual effectiveness to children through our Kids of the Kingdom program Sundays and Wednesdays.

I. The Ministry of the Body of the Congregation

"The reason we are growing as a congregation is because we are learning that we are all ministers," noted one of our men. II Corinthians 3:5,6 points out that believers have a built-in sufficiency for the ministry of New Testament vitality. The Lord, who has worked a literal masterpiece (Eph. 2:10, *poiema*) in each of us, wills to accomplish His good pleasure through us (Phil. 2:13).

The removal of the hierarchical structure in the church is not brutal iconoclasm: it is simply scriptural reality. Neither is the emphasis on every believer's ministry a reduction of the place given by the Lord Jesus Christ to the various ministries of Ephesians 4:11. Those ministries are basic to the cultivation of a ministering church, and each of them has its God-ordained place of authority. But "authority" is not prestige or position in the human sense of the word. It is rooted in the Word and communicated in the power of the Holy Spirit. This authority does not assert itself to the wilting of those it influences, but accomplishes the strengthening of those who are to learn their place of authority and ministry in the functioning Body of Jesus. This initial principle of developing the ministry of the whole Body of the local church is best verbalized by my friend, Jerry Cook, pastor of a sister-church to ours in Gresham, Oregon: "God hasn't called us to build big churches, but to build big people; and big people seem to have a way of building big churches."

II. The Freedom of Service under the Holy Spirit Guidance

"I would say it's best seen in the unstructured form of service we experience. The pastor even sometimes forgets to take the offering." So observed another of our councilmen, and the neglected offering is not something reveled in for any selfish reasons. Rather, the comment gives indication that there have been times when our overriding concern that ministry be accomplished in other areas of operation has brought us to the end of the service without even noticing that the offering was overlooked. Another said, "We are more concerned about what we are doing than in how we do it."

But the point is found in the absence of structure in the services. To some, the suggestion of a relaxed, informal mode of worship conjures up images of disorder, incoherence, confusion, and turmoil. Others might hasten to defend the fact that structure may be planned prayerfully and, therefore, be spiritually sound. To these, we simply respond that neither fear of confusion nor contention about planning have any place in the situation God has permitted us to enjoy. When the leadership knows the Word, and the assembled body regards the Word, there is a liberty within scriptural limits which allows for a gracious, tasteful, charming work of the Holy Spirit glorifying Jesus Christ. With regularity, people receive Christ as Savior, are healed, baptized in the Holy Spirit, during the process of the entire service, not only at some climactic point or invitation appeal.

Each meeting has a similarity to others that is as marked with evidence of design as a leaf or a snowflake, and yet with the identifiable uniqueness which each of these has from others of its kind. The basic ingredients of the Hour of Worship and Ministry (the Sunday morning service, ordinarily nearly two hours in length) are praise, singing, interaction in prayer and conversation, teaching in the Word of God, and exhortation. The chemistry of each service is worked out by the Holy Spirit, acknowledged Leader of these assembly times. He combines the ingredients in new and living ways so that regular exercises of worship are kept fresh by His innovative use of them.

III. The Abiding Sense of Loving Fellowship in the Spirit.

"The man who visited with our family recently said he couldn't get over the sense of love that filled the place." This comment reflects a whole bevy of remarks such as: "There is a willingness to accept everyone—we have straight conservatives and long-haired street-type Christians worshiping together, loving one another, and growing together in Christ"; "The unity and singleness of accord—it's like Acts 2, I guess"; "The lady we brought was quite apprehensive in coming, knowing ours was a Pentecostal church; but she departed saying it was the closest thing to true worship which she would think possible."

Another stated, "When you pray with people, together, in concern for their need, it produces a continuing sense of love—a caring, and sharing together of our life in Jesus. Ministry-time is a key part of the spirit of love we enjoy."

So that the priceless presence of the Holy Spirit not be grieved, we have committed ourselves as a church to a sane, sensible, and sensitive walk and worship in the Holy Spirit. We consider it essential to identify and to school the congregation regarding the varied manifestations of the Holy Spirit and the practices of Spirit-filled saints. The operation of the gifts, the timeless, scriptural practices of worship—upraised hands, verbalized praise, clapping of hands, singing, etc.—are not only experienced, they are explained. This accomplishes several things, notably: (1) an intelligent body of worshippers, participating with understanding and awareness, and thereby with power; (2) the reclamation of any disenchanted Pentecostals who have lost appreciation for these practices because of their past perfunctory participation; and (3) the assisting of the uninitiated into New Testament practices toward a sense of comfort and rejoicing in the presence of God.

Contrary to the average Pentecostal thinking of the traditional past, we believe that the supernatural work of God should make people feel comfortable, not at ease in their sin, but giving an assuring sense of the Lord's dynamic presence to lift them by His love.

Roy Hicks, with whose church in Eugene, Oregon, we share much in the life of the Holy Spirit, has put it cogently: "The youth culture of our day has, I think, helped us to understand the word 'supernatural.' In their vernacular, things that are special are 'super'—super-neat, super-hard, super-good, super-wild, etc. For my part, I think the glory of God at work among his people is intended to help people to be super-natural; that is, to rise to the level of real, liberated manhood or womanhood, truly 'natural' according to God's original design for man."

This super-naturalness worked by the Holy Spirit among us, is causing people to love, love in the solid, biblical, "agape" sense of the word. We refuse to be deceived by the cheap, humanistic imitation of "luv" at this present world's level.

One last aspect of the work of God's love among us is difficult for sincere traditionalists to accept. Although we teach a strong message leading to growth and the grasping of truth which will cultivate practical holiness, we do not condemn new believers—or long-term ones for that matter—for instances of failure in areas of life where the full experience of sanctification has not yet been realized. Naturally, the clear teaching of Scripture is contended for in all areas of integrity, character, and morality.

But this is balanced by a love which covers sin (I Pet. 4:8) and leads to strength, instead of pointing out failure, which tends to produce a binding of souls with a spirit of condemnation. In so brief a commentary there is no space to make a defense against potential accusations of "cheap grace," but we know whereof we speak and are sure of the Holy Spirit of love leading us in this challenging aspect of reality in Christ the Lord.

The principles summarized are simply that the work has been built by the Lord Jesus Christ, teaching us (1) to cultivate the ministry of the body of the church; (2) to learn to worship and minister as directed by the superintending work of the Holy Spirit; and (3) to speak the truth in love, permitting the same Spirit to lead us deeper and deeper into this "more excellent way."

A New England New Testament Church

Peter J. Marshall

The small clapboard-covered colonial-style church is on a quiet tree-shaded street in a quaint little village of old captains' houses on Cape Cod. Sometimes the only sounds to break the afternoon's stillness are the cries of the sea gulls as they wheel over the steeple. The East Dennis Community Church is the type of church that makes tourists reach for their cameras. But there is another story to the place that cannot be told in photographs.

I inherited a congregation that was small, hopelessly unspiritual, and rather completely bound up in New England traditionalism. It consisted mainly of older people who were firmly set in what was an arch-conservative semirural society. Sermon topics from days of yore included "Cranberry Picking on Cape Cod," and some folks still remember the Sunday when the organist played "Home on the Range" for the offertory anthem!

Humanly, it is impossible to come to a church like that and see it revolutionized into a growing, evangelical, financially dynamic, missions-oriented congregation made up of people of all ages, with many of them really excited about the life in Jesus Christ and experiencing the charismatic gifts of the Holy Spirit-but without backbiting and schism. There is absolutely no way any pastor or any group of people could achieve this. Yet this is precisely what has happened here at our church during the last four years.

I stand in awe of what God has done. The credit belongs completely to God—Father, Son, and Holy Spirit. The East Dennis Church seems to have been chosen by Jesus Christ to prove that the miracle of church revival can happen today, that He does choose the most hopeless situations in which to do it, and that He has not simply "written off" the spiritually dead churches in our land. Jesus Christ is in the business of resurrection!

Oh, there were many days when I didn't believe that even He could do it. We were tempted to leave for "greener pastures" so often. But the Lord provided us with fellowship and spiritual feeding at the Community of Jesus near us in Orleans, and this helped us greatly in the dark moments.

And then, the Lord provided us with a glimmer of hope and encouragement every once in a while, a counseling breakthrough with someone or a good small-group fellowship meeting on Sunday night, or perhaps a new family that was beginning to get interested in the Lord Jesus and what He was doing among us. Little did I understand that out of the few people who came to me for counseling that first year would come several strong church members for the years ahead and that this would become a recurring pattern.

I was the neediest. That of course, was Lesson No. 1. The Lord still had to show me that one of the persons most in need in the church was me. Why had He allowed me to be brought into this god-forsaken situation? Why had He allowed me to be deceived into thinking that this church was ready to roll spiritually when 90 percent of the people didn't know a blessed thing about what it means to be born again in Christ . . . not to mention anything about the Holy Spirit?

Why? Because He wanted to deal individually with my wife and myself. I am convinced that God fits churches to pastors just as carefully as He fits pastors to churches. We all get in life what we need to force us to grow up and change, to get-with becoming the persons we're supposed to be.

There are no accidents for a Christian. In order to be obedient to God and reflect the glory of Jesus Christ, I must die to the desire to be successful as a pastor, lest I be guilty of the ghastly sin of building a kingdom around myself, rather than around Jesus. God will put us in situations where others do not accept our leadership or what we preach from the pulpit.

And, we have to learn that God puts us into these predicaments deliberately, to force us to ensure that it is the Holy Spirit preaching through us and exercising pastoral oversight through us.

We pastors can gather followers without realizing it and build churches on the basis of our personalities and talents instead of on the basis of *who Jesus is.* We have to recognize this temptation and renounce it, just as Jesus did (Matt. 4:7-10). It is Jesus that people need, not pastors. So many of my pastor brethren are caught in this trap. If people won't listen to them, then they "shake the dust off their feet" and go where there are those who are "really hungry for the Gospel."

What a strong temptation! And yet, in giving in, we take ourselves from the very situation that God has carefully constructed to force us to grow and change. God is more concerned with us as individuals than He is with our "ministries." The real ministry flows from what Christ is doing in us, not what we're trying to do for Christ.

I had to lean weakly against the doorway of the sanctuary and pray that Jesus would have mercy upon me and the people, keeping me out of the way so He could shine through. I had to learn that my worst problem in the church was not problem people, it was me.

If we are willing to stay in the situation God has placed us in or permitted us to enter into, instead of getting out, or switching churches, or getting divorced, or resigning, or something else, and if we will deal with the "log in our own eye" (Matt. 7:3)—our haughtiness and pride, our desire to be thought well of, having always to be right, having to be loved, adulated, and adored, our lack of compassion, our critical spirit and refusal to truly forgive—then God will move with great power in the situation. But not until we come to repentance.

As I struggled with my own sinful nature, and my resentment against those who were resisting both my pastoral leadership and Jesus Christ and His Gospel, God began to honor even my initial desire to die to self.

As the first summer waxed hotter, it became readily apparent that the church was being overwhelmed with hordes of people eager to hear the Gospel message. The situation came to be rather humorous actually, because we crammed people in every way we could think of, even to having the teenagers sit in the aisles. And still they came.

One hot August Sunday, we had people sitting in the ladies' restroom with the door open, and the ushers were silently hoping the fire marshal was spending the day on the beach. Even a minimal response of repentance, it seems, is enough to get things started.

Meanwhile, however, the "old guard" was increasingly unhappy over the crowds, the changes in the old ways of doing things, and the content of the evangelical sermons. Finally, the whole matter came to a congregational vote over whether or not I would stay on as pastor. We won the vote by a very narrow margin—perhaps because, like David of old, I gave in to the temptation to count the troops on "the Lord's side."

Thereafter, without our yet having any power in the church to change anything, God himself really began to alter matters. Those who had been opposed to the preaching of the Gospel and to the emergence of the church into an evangelical fellowship suddenly disappeared. It was as if a literal fulfillment of Scripture (Isa. 49:19-21) had occurred, one, in fact, that was given to us as a word of prophecy on a Sunday evening at our fellowship meeting.

Next, the Holy Spirit prompted the "antis" to resign from the church boards, so suddenly that in a matter of two months the way was cleared to develop a whole new leadership team of people committed to Christ.

During the same period, the Lord had begun to send us people who were really hungry for the Gospel of Jesus Christ. They came from everywhere, often from distances that were several hours' drive away. One middle-aged couple, church members all their lives but never born anew through Jesus Christ, began coming regularly. They received Christ as their Lord and Savior, were baptized in the Holy Spirit, and baptized by immersion in water, and have since become two of our strongest church members. They reside more than an hour's drive from the church.

Not only has our Sunday-morning attendance continued to grow, but there has been a vast turnover in the actual membership. Our parish now stretches over a hundred miles, with many people making real sacrifices of time and effort to come.

Some of our older church members have experienced spiritual renewal in their lives, too. There have been fewer of these, but they have produced some poignant moments during the last four years.

There was the bright and sparkling afternoon I led one of our eighty-year-old grandmothers down into the waters of Bass River to be baptized while the speedboats circled, wondering what in the world was going on. She had experienced Jesus as her Savior, personally alive for her, after years of nominal church membership as a preacher's daughter.

With these experiences has come a growing desire on the part of many to really put the biblical principles of the Body of Christ into action. For example, we have become convinced that the key to a church's financial success is twofold:

First, to proclaim Jesus Christ as Lord and Savior in a personal way and to trust Him to draw all men to himself. Our experience has been that when men and women find Jesus Christ as the real answer to their needs, they will give financially at the place where they are finding Him.

Secondly, we have discovered that God means for the biblical principle-commandment of tithing to apply to churches as well as individuals. The oft-heard cry, "I can't afford to tithe," is beginning to give way to the cry, "I can't afford not to tithe."

The more our church gives to missions, the more God blesses the church. His demonstrations of this has been nothing short of miraculous. The percentage of missions' money in our budget has grown in four years from 6 percent to around 40 percent. Incredibly, it shows no signs of stopping or even tapering off. In turn, God has really honored our commitment to the mission work of Christ in the world and so blessed our church financially that we have actually oversubscribed our annual budget for the past four years.

Another of the most basic biblical principles for the Body of Christ which we have sought to put into action has been the idea of living according to the discipline of real commitment to Christ in all things. In order to join our church, a prospective member must profess a real experience of rebirth through personal surrender to Jesus as Lord and Savior. In addition, there must be a genuine commitment to being an individual member of the Body of Christ in our congregation in terms of time, money, and desire for real, genuine fellowship. This requirement has slowed our growth rate somewhat, but a few deeply dedicated Christians are worth dozens of nominal ones.

Lastly, we are concerned about getting inside each other's lives and truly becoming "members of one another." This involves the pain of real honesty with each other and the willingness to submit ourselves to words of correction. But what deep love Jesus brings us when we're willing to take these risks!

Not all of us at the church are so involved, but those who come to grips with our need to grow into Jesus Christ emotionally, mentally, and spiritually are experiencing the creation of a rich life together in Christ. We are beginning to learn what the Greek word for fellowship — *koinonia* — really means.

The miracle is not nearly completed. There is still much change needed in all of us at East Dennis Community Church. We must be patient and accept the fact that even the true church of Jesus Christ is at least partly institutional — and made up wholly of sinners.

One of the greatest revelations God has given me in my life with Christ is that our Heavenly Father is not in the business of reforming institutions but of redeeming individuals. If we concentrate on furthering Christ's redeeming work on the inside of people, they will eventually come to the point of revitalizing the structure of their own church. If one recognizes this truth and accepts it, he can live and work in the institutional church without bitterness.

If the Lord Jesus can begin to work His miracle of resurrection in our midst, He can do it anywhere.

A Southern New Testament Church

Jamie Buckingham

It sounds like wind moving gently through the leaves of a forest. It is the sound of people worshipping.

Three hundred people have gathered in a simple concrete-block building. All kinds of people: a rough-looking man with bulging muscles, a bearded ex-drug addict, a college boy with short hair, a dignified woman in an expensive suit, a beautiful blonde in jeans and sweatshirt, a black man with a bristling Afro, a young mother with four children, a radiant middle-aged businessman—all are sitting together on folding chairs with heads bowed or upraised, praising God.

It is eleven o'clock Sunday morning, the time some clergymen have called "the deadest hour of the week." But there's life here, in this building known simply as a tabernacle, located on the east coast of Florida at the southern tip of Cape Kennedy.

The sound waxes and wanes. Silence. Then spontaneously, the people break into a simple song. The strongest voice is that of a former professor of music at a Southern Baptist seminary who was led to move to the town of Melbourne "on faith," trusting God to provide for him and his family as he ministers in the local Body of Christ. The harmony sounds like a giant choir as the people sing, "He is Lord, He is Lord. He is risen from the dead and He is Lord..."

Then the tempo changes. The sound of tambourine and piano join the handclapping crowd as they sing verse after verse from the Scriptures, concluding with Psalm 63: "Thy lovingkindness is better than life... I will lift up my hands in thy name." All over the room, hands are extended upward in worship.

There is silence again. A man speaks haltingly, "My people, hear my voice . . ." It is prophecy. As he finishes, a murmur of assent wafts through the room. Another man speaks. He is a former minister with the Church of God, Anderson, Indiana, who has ministered in the local Body of Christ for more than six years. Like all the other ministers or elders, he receives no salary, simply trusting the Lord for enough offerings to provide his needs. He speaks, this time in a language that sounds like a mixture of French and Hebrew. Someone murmurs, "Give us your interpretation, Lord." Silence. Then a woman speaks. She is a Roman Catholic housewife whose husband is an engineer at the nearby Space Center. "My children, stand fast upon my Word. Heed not those who mix My blood with water . . ."

More silence. Then there is music—angelic, ethereal. It starts softly from the far corner of the room where a Presbyterian elder is sitting with his wife and family. It floats across the room as many voices blend in singing songs of praises. The words are sometimes understandable, "Hallelujah! Praise God!" but more often in strange languages. The sound rises and falls like waves on a gentle sea as each voice sings solo praise, yet in perfect harmony like a majestic orchestra under the Master Conductor.

A man rises with a Bible in his hand. He is a former Methodist who gave up his job as a prospering stockbroker to devote his full time to ministry. He preaches an impassioned sermon, speaking about ten minutes and then sitting down.

Another man rises to his feet. He is a local building contractor. "Last night in my quiet time the Lord spoke to me, giving me these Scriptures to share with the Body today."

Another song, this time from the Baptist Hymnal, as the majestic strains of "A Mighty Fortress Is Our God" roll heavenward. Then an offering. Before the plates are passed, a simple announcement is made.

"This Body of Christians has no membership, nor does it have a budget. If the Lord leads you to designate your offering, please so do. All gifts that are not designated will be prayed over by a group of men who will seek the Lord's will for distribution. None of it will be held in savings; every penny goes immediately into ministry. If anyone here has a need, we urge you to take out of the plate as it is passed. Others will be giving twice as much while some will give all they have."

The offering is a joyous affair, with most of the giving in cash. Occasionally a diamond ring will appear in the offering plate. Then a former Southern Baptist pastor stands. "The Holy Spirit has told me there are several persons here who have never made a public profession of their faith in Jesus Christ. Jesus says to confess Him publicly. We now give you that opportunity."

What seems like an eternity of silence passes, but all over the room hundreds of lips are moving in silent prayer. Then a man rises from the congregation and with much emotion says, "Today I want to declare my stand for Jesus Christ." The room bursts into rejoicing and the sound of hosannas is mixed with warm applause. Another man rises to his feet. "I've been a member of a church for thirty years but have never said publicly that Jesus is my Savior." A hippie-looking girl stands and tries to speak, but her body is shaking with emotion. Immediately four or five others rise and stand with her, laying on hands and praying. Suddenly she breaks forth in praise shouting, "I give my life to Jesus!" Others stand to lay hands on her, and moments later she bursts forth in tongues as her newfound Savior baptizes her in the Holy Spirit.

By this time, the altar is filled with kneeling people, some receiving healing, some seeking salvation, others being baptized in the Holy Spirit. All are being ministered to by members of the Body who come forward spontaneously to lay on hands, pray, and counsel.

Even though the service lasts almost two hours, when the final prayer is said the people still linger, counseling at the altar, praying in a back room, drinking coffee from a nearby urn, or just standing around hugging each other. A stranger whispers to his neighbor, "I've never seen such love."

The neighbor replies, "It must be Jesus."

But is wasn't always like this. Four years ago the church was a normal, struggling Southern Baptist church looking for new concepts of church renewal. However, the people had committed themselves to a trust relationship with each other and their pastor and were determined to study the Bible to find the secrets of spiritual power.

Then the pastor, attending a regional convention of the Full Gospel Business Men's Fellowship, received the baptism in the Holy Spirit. He returned to the church and told them what he had experienced. Although the people knew nothing of the Baptism in the Holy Spirit or spiritual gifts, they recognized it as scriptural and therefore valid. The search was on.

Gradually it became apparent that there were others in the city of Melbourne who had received the same experience. Since they were not allowed to exercise their new joy in the institutional churches, they were worshipping in small home groups. They had called a former Church of God minister who had been ousted from his denomination because he spoke in tongues as their leader. A former Methodist youth director, a mother with three children, was also teaching this group of charismatics. Both leaders were supported by love offerings only.

When the word spread that a Baptist church was now beginning to walk in the Spirit, the interdenominational group began attending the services. Realizing the need for teaching, the pastor and deacons of the Baptist Church invited the leaders of the other group to preach and hold classes. Bit by bit, most of the Baptists received the baptism in the Holy Spirit and began to exercise the gifts of the Spirit in the church service.

Then came freedom. The printed order of service was thrown away. All services were Spirit-led. The Baptist remnant met, and after fasting and praying for a week, decided to drop the name Baptist and simply be Jesus People. A week later, the church was voted out of the local Baptist association — a move which proved to be the key to allow other charismatics from all over the area to come and worship freely.

By common consent, the membership roll and all attendance records were destroyed. The pastor, now serving as just one of several elders in the flock, said, "We are to invite people to join the Kingdom of God, not some man-made institution. When a local body sets itself up as an end rather than a means, and demands loyalty to the institution, then it becomes an idol and must be cast down."

All the old offices and committees were dissolved, and the people determined they would have no officers, no elders or deacons, until the Lord specifically directed. The budget was laid aside, and all money began going immediately into ministry as the Lord directed on a week-by-week basis. In a short while, the offerings and the crowd tripled in size.

A former Southern Baptist seminary professor who held a secular job in the city announced that the Lord was calling him to British Honduras as a missionary. A Canadian couple, former independent missionaries in South America who had been sent back to the States because they spoke in tongues, announced that the Lord was telling them to return to Brazil. A young Presbyterian, an engineer with an aerospace industry, announced that the Lord was telling him to resign his job and go to Brazil to preach. All left without a promise of any financial support, but trusting God to supply their needs — most of which are being met through the local Body in Melbourne.

A boys' house, "His House," ministering to drug users and runaways, was opened and directed by an ex-schoolteacher. Later it evolved into a training school for youth, directed by another former Southern Baptist pastor and an ex-alcoholic. A former Methodist pastor and his wife opened a youth ranch west of town and began ministering to homeless boys and girls by taking them into their home. Many other families began doing the same thing with just one or two homeless youths or troubled people moving in on temporary schedules. A bookstore was opened in the business district, and later a branch opened on the beach. One of the men in the Body invested much of his savings to purchase sophisticated tape recording and reproducing machines, and soon tapes of the teachers in the local Body and visiting speakers were being sent out all over the nation to those who requested them.

People began driving in from miles around to attend the Believers' Meetings, as the Sunday meetings were called. Home prayer groups met morning and night through the week, with ministry in deliverance, healing, and evangelism. Many of those attending were still active in various denominational churches, coming to the Belivers' Meetings or prayer groups for spiritual food and fellowship. Others felt led to break free from the denominational church and devote their full ministry to the local Body of Christ. However, excellent rapport was maintained with many of the local denominational ministers since no one was ever encouraged to leave his church. Although there were many problems, the theme, "We are one in the Spirit," prevailed — and still does.

Recently a Pentecostal pastor from another state drove to Melbourne to spend a week observing the ministry. On the Monday he was to leave, he stopped by the New Life Book House for a cup of coffee. Seeing one of the men in the local Body come in to purchase a book, he asked, "When did you people have your last revival meeting?"

The man thought for a moment and said, "Yesterday morning."

"Oh," the visiting pastor said. "How long has it lasted?"

"Four years," the man said, "and it's just getting started."

A Western New Testament Church

John P. French

Stained-glass windows, comfortable pews with kneelers, a large asphalt parking lot — none of them make a church as the Bible defines the church. Indeed, if you were standing on Invergordon Road in Scottsdale, Arizona, looking at Calvary Church of the Valley, you might think it looked considerably more like a motel than a church edifice as we have come to know one.

Calvary Church came into being when some thirty families from an Episcopal church in the area asked an Episcopal priest from New York City — by way of Colorado and Arizona — to join with them in forming the new church. It's one doctrine: the Bible as the total and complete Word of God. They pledged enough money to run the new church for two years, and applied to the Episcopal diocese to become a member. However, this request was turned down by the diocese after much discussion, and Calvary began to function as an independent church, totally dependent on our Lord Jesus Christ and the guidance of His Holy Spirit. And that is the way it is today.

At the beginning, probably no more than 10 percent of the men involved had received the baptism in the Holy Spirit, and some 50 percent really knew nothing about it. But because Richard Zollner, the Episcopal priest who was our spiritual leader, and his wife had received the Spirit some seven years earlier, the hunger for this greater gift from God spread rapidly. So rapidly, in fact, that by the end of the first year the percentages had about reversed themselves, with no more than 10 percent of those active in the church NOT baptized with the Holy Spirit.

For the first ten months of its emerging life, Calvary met once a week in a convention room at a Scottsdale resort and during the week in private homes. Attendance ran in the neighborhood of 100 at first, and often considerably lower. Some new people came, some of the original ones left. Indeed, it was very much like shifting sand, and no one was at all sure what the Lord was doing with Calvary.

The day of reckoning came when, at the regular monthly vestry meeting, the treasurer announced that the bank account was down to forty-two cents. We hurried over the list of pledges, trying to find out who wasn't paying, who perhaps had departed, why a family hadn't been present the past two Sundays—in short, we applied all of the man-made systems we had learned in years of church activity in the mainline churches.

But then the Lord really moved upon that vestry meeting and the group of twelve men who made up that body went down on their knees and committed the entire problem to the Lord. If there really was some reason why He did not want this new church to exist, then we didn't want it either. We just asked Him to go ahead and let the bank account get on down to zero, and we would close up shop.

At the same time, we were led to take two major actions to back up our commitment to Him: (1) we gave up all pledging, depending entirely on the Lord to provide, without every-member canvasses or sales tactics to get the dollars in; and (2) we began to tithe everything that came in to the church, giving the first 10 percent of every dollar to the mission field. By the mission field, I mean the spreading of the Gospel of Jesus Christ at home and abroad.

Immediately after the announcement was made the following Sunday, the Lord began to provide. Since that day there has never been a time when there were not sufficient funds to meet every need. But that wasn't all. Within two weeks we were shown a piece of real estate which we were witnessed to as just the place the Lord meant to be the permanent home of Calvary Church of the Valley.

A former resort, it sat on five acres in the heart of the residential area of Scottsdale — Paradise Valley. There was a large lodge, suitable for the main church building. In addition, there were seventeen living units. Again the vestry met, this time on our knees as at the beginning. And again we came out with action — an offer to the owner to buy this property under a very unusual plan: $15,000 down (the date was the week of Thanksgiving,); an additional $35,000 by December 31st; and the remaining $80,000 by December 31st, the following year, making a total price of $130,000 all at no interest if payments were made on time. Otherwise, interest was to be paid retroactively on the total amount.

Not too much to our surprise (since we knew we had been led by God in the matter), the proposal was accepted. We had on hand $15,000 given us for land purchase with which we made the down payment. The rest was on faith. Again the announcement in church, again no canvass or fund-raising drive. We received $1,000 more than was needed for the payment due December 31st. During the next year, the money came in to meet the additional $80,000, plus another $15,000 for repairs and installation of air-conditioning. No single gift was more than $10,000 either year.

Although it was originally a resort motel, the complex has proved to be beautifully laid out for service as a New Testament church. There is a large swimming pool, said to be "the largest baptismal font in the state of Arizona." Six of the seventeen living units are used as quarters for staff members and the family of Pastor Zollner. One room functions as a prayer chapel, others as Sunday-school rooms, with two rooms set aside for visiting speakers and occasions when a person needing spiritual help comes to stay overnight.

Financially, the Lord has continued to bless Calvary. Our operating expenses run about $35,000 per year. Since there is no planned income, there is no budget. In addition, we are giving nearly twice this amount of money to missions. As special needs have come up, they have been met. All of this has been done with no fund-raising campaigns.

The only mention of finances, ever, is a paragraph in the Sunday bulletin explaining that we do not make pledges at Calvary but are entirely dependent on the Lord, knowing He will provide for the needs He wants met. Indeed, the majority of our regular people (it is hard to talk about members, because with no pledges they are difficult to identify as such) tithe or better. As of this writing, the church is holding a sizable surplus. We are waiting for the Lord to reveal His purpose for it.

The Lord has also enlarged the outreach of the property considerably. Services of various types have evolved to meet almost every need. Every morning there is about an hour of intercessory prayer. The Sunday morning Bible study and church service are still pretty much our outreach service. Occasionally the gifts will be manifested there, and we do make available a time for Body ministry at the conclusion, but the service is totally unthreatening to newcomers.

Sunday and Thursday evenings are Spirit-led prayer and praise meetings where the gifts operate freely and the Body ministry comes into heavy use. Tuesday evening there are three different types of Bible study, from beginners to a very advanced course. The women's Bible study is on a Thursday morning, and an informal Holy Communion, sharing, and Body ministry service is held on Wednesday morning. It is attended by people from churches from all over the Valley. Every other week it is led by the pastor, on alternate weeks by a layman. The men's breakfast is also on Thursday mornings. And on Friday evening, an inquirer's class on the baptism in the Holy Spirit meets — Scripture is explained, and the baptism is ministered to those desiring it.

In all these areas, however, there is no attempt to proselyte members for Calvary Church. We have had ministers from at least three denominations come to learn about, and subsequently received, the baptism in the Holy Spirit at Calvary. Likewise, visiting members from at least twenty denominations that we know of are fed at one or more of these services.

Other missionary outreaches of the church include the Calvary library which mails books all over the country and maintains a lending library for the area, and a tract ministry which has distributed throughout the U.S. almost 15,000 copies of *After You Receive the Baptism in the Holy Spirit.* The Calvary tape-of-the-month plan supplies hundreds with cassette recorders and selected tapes featuring prominent speakers in the charismatic movement.

Many fine speakers have been brought to the area, speaking in the church itself and, where more room was needed, at other locations. With spiritual growth have come problems, too, but we find that as we become better equipped to fight spiritual problems with spiritual weapons, those problems don't really seem so difficult. Growth is provided for all God's people.

Only the Lord knows where Calvary is going. All we do is trust Him completely, to try and never lose sight of the fact that it is His church and not ours, and praise Him in everything.

An English New Testament Church

Michael Darwood

My employment brought me to live in a small English village called Hemingford Grey some years ago. At that time, my wife and I were typical church-going heathens and we stayed that way for our first few years. Apart from a small Congregational Church that held a service every other Sunday evening, the only place of worship at Hemingford was St. James' Parish Church. So, there we went. The Vicar said later he was at that time saved and still preaching the Gospel, but he no longer expected anything to happen.

I was to learn, however, that we had arrived in Hemingford just as the Lord began to move by sending Christians of various denominations and nationalities to live in the area. Most of them began to worship at St. James Church. Before long, the Vicar found himself under pressure to start a mid-week Prayer Meeting and, when he gave way on the matter, it was proposed that a Mission should be held in the village. Again, he fought the idea, all he wanted at that time was a quiet life. But, eventually, he was defeated and the Mission was held.

In preparation for the Mission, every home was visited in the village to invite people to the meetings. A Christian named David Laycock was assigned the street on which we were living. He had been a Christian for several years and often talked to people about the Lord, but found himself unable to lead them right through to a personal knowledge of the Lord Jesus Christ. Just prior to the Hemingford Mission, David attended a crusade conducted by Evangelist Don Double in the nearby town of Huntingdon. There, he received the baptism in the Holy Spirit and spoke in other tongues.

He did not mention this to anyone but when he began visiting for the Mission he noticed a change in his ministry. He was led to concentrate on a home opposite our own, the residence of Roy and Elizabeth Peacock, and by the end of the Mission they both had accepted Christ as Savior. He knew then that the baptism in the Holy Spirit was real. A number of follow-up house meetings were planned after the Mission, and the Peacocks asked if one could be held at their home with David as leader. This was agreed but David suggested they should not invite people to the meetings, rather, just wait to see what the Lord would do.

Although my wife and I had been hardly touched by the Mission, a question began to nag at us both about that time: "What is a Christian?" It all had begun during the previous Feast of Pentecost when my son, who was 13 and attending a church youth group, went to a special outreach meeting on Saturday evening. On Sunday morning, I was cleaning shoes in the kitchen when Graham came in and I questioned him about the meeting. He told me about the food and drinks he had enjoyed, about the singing group and their guitars, and how after the meeting a man spoke to him about Jesus Christ. The man asked him if he was a Christian and he said, "No." I thought this was strange but Graham went on to say, "Then he asked me if you and mother were Christians and I said, 'No. You were not Christians either.'"

This made me mad and I really told Graham off for daring to intimate we were heathens. Of course, we were Christians. Did we not go to church? Had we not been baptized and confirmed? But from that time on we were constantly aware of the unanswered question: "What is a Christian? And also, are we Christians?"

Then, quite casually, we heard of the house meetings starting across the way and asked if we could go. Maybe we would discover the answers to our questions there. In various ways, the Holy Spirit led others to that first meeting at the Peacock's home. Without inviting anyone they had a full house. Within a few weeks my wife and I both discovered what a Christian was and became Christians. David now found that whenever he spoke to anyone about the Lord Jesus, something happened. Soon, all those in the group had either accepted Christ or rejected His offer of salvation and stopped attending the meetings.

About a month after our conversion, Evangelist Don Double returned to Huntingdon for some "Deeper Life" meetings. David Laycock thought it would be a good idea to take the group along. He expected we would be told to read our Bibles, pray regularly, attend church meetings, and get involved in church activities; instead, the evangelist spoke on the baptism in the Holy Spirit. Although we had never heard of this before, three of us received the baptism in the Holy Spirit, and spoke in other tongues, by the time the meetings ended. The others came into the blessing soon afterwards.

It was just before Christmas that year when my wife and I knelt at the communion rail of the little Baptist Church where Don was preaching. We had been told that soon someone would come and pray with us and we would then be baptized in the Holy Spirit, and speak in other tongues. Before anyone could minister to us, however, the Holy Spirit fell on us and, although we had never heard anyone else speak in other tongues, we both began to praise God in a new language.

We went home rejoicing at what the Lord had done. But, by bedtime, my wife had developed one of her migraine headaches. These usually lasted for two or three days and were really painful. As she told me about the attack, I felt the compassion of the Lord well up within me and I laid my hand on her head and said, "I am sorry." Later when I asked her how she felt she said that when I laid my hand on her head the pain went away. Since that time she has never had another migraine headache; the Lord healed her completely. Our first reaction to the miracle was fear and wonder. What had happened? No one we asked could help us and we could not find any books on the subject to read. But Don Double had referred us to 1 Corinthians, chapters 12 to 14, in his message, and we turned to that part of the Bible for help. We came to the conclusion we had experienced a manifestation of the power of the Holy Spirit in the "Gift of Healing."

Our small group met regularly for prayer, Bible study and fellowship and, as we were praying one evening, Elizabeth Peacock suddenly began to pray aloud in a strange tongue. We all opened our eyes and sat up. We had been told to pray in our new tongues daily in our private devotions but this was something new. Then my wife, Muriel, said, "As Elizabeth was speaking, I knew what she was saying." We turned to Paul's first letter to the Corinthians and decided this must be "tongues and interpretation." It was agreed that the next time Elizabeth spoke aloud in tongues, Muriel would tell us what the message meant. This happened a few days later but as Muriel tried to interpret while Elizabeth was still speaking, the result was confusing. So, we read the Scriptures and prayed again and suggested that next time Muriel should wait until Elizabeth had finished before she started. This resulted in blessing, the Holy Spirit had introduced us to two more of His *gifts*.

Another evening, as we were seeking the Lord's will on a particular matter, David shared that some words kept impressing themselves on him. We turned to 1 Corinthians and felt this could be prophecy. It was suggested that we return to prayer and that David speak out the words. As he did so, more words came. Slowly and with some hesitation, he brought us a wonderful message of comfort and exhortation from the Lord.

Shortly after this, my wife visited a girl who had received Christ the previous day and who seemed to have some sort of inner conflict. My wife sent an *arrow prayer* to the Lord and received the instructions, "Ask her what will happen about her Muslim boy friend now she is a Christian?" Muriel put the question and the girl asked how she knew about the Muslim boy friend. Muriel replied that the Lord had just told her. The matter was dealt with and eventually the girl married a Christian man. The Lord had introduced us to another of the gifts of the Spirit, namely, the Word of Knowledge.

In this way, all the nine gifts of the Spirit mentioned in 1 Corinthians 12 to 14 came into operation in the group. But we were not without our problems. Most of the local Christians were very disturbed at our experience and we were warned we had gone into error, or even that we were demon-possessed. Leaflets were pushed into our mail boxes telling us of the dreadful things that happened to people who spoke in other tongues. We were no longer so welcome at the mid-week prayer meetings. No doubt the Vicar was equally disturbed by what was happening but he realized the importance of keeping us in fellowship in the church, rather than letting us be driven away to form a holy huddle. Thanks to his love and wisdom, this did not happen.

The following Spring, a visiting speaker attended our home meeting and we invited the Vicar. We all waited for some reaction from him but none came. Next morning, a Saturday, as David was praying, he saw a vision of the Vicar kneeling by the lectern with praying hands and a scroll above his head bearing the words, *Behold he prayeth.* David felt the Lord was impressing him to pray with the Vicar to receive the baptism in the Holy Spirit. But his first reaction was that no one less than a Bishop could pray for a Vicar. All day he wrestled with the problem and finally, late in the evening, he went to the Vicarage. The Vicar was in his study, preparing for his sermon for the next morning. The ground floor study had a door opening directly onto the garden. He called this his "Nicodemus door" and here David came secretly, by night, to explain that he believed the Lord would have him pray with the Vicar to receive the baptism in the Holy Spirit. To his surprise the Vicar replied, "Then, pray." This raised another problem, however, as David had no idea how to pray. He laid his hands on the Vicar's head and prayed a simple prayer. The Vicar began to speak in other tongues and David went home to bed.

Next morning my wife and I went to church wondering what had happened. As soon as the Vicar began to preach, we knew. As people walked down the church path after the service they were saying to each other, "What has happened to the Vicar? His sermon was different this morning." Praise God. His sermons have been different ever since.

Since then, I have left Hemingford to join Don Double and the Good News Crusade team in Cornwall. Recently, I visited Hemingford to speak at a house meeting and found that the Holy Spirit is still at work there. Some 40 teenagers have been saved and are communicating the Gospel in the surrounding villages. During the meeting, there was a prophecy that the blessings that began at Hemingford and that have been radiating out from this village since then, are just waiting to be released so that they can pour out across the surrounding countryside. Even so, do it Lord.

A Scottish New Testament Church

Jim Handyside

One starlit night in 1950, a young man, recently converted in the army, climbed a local hill and gazed down on Clydebank, Scotland, a town of 50,000 inhabitants. There he and his companion prayed that the mighty God he had newly come to know would spare the city and raise a real testimony in its midst.

With half the population Roman Catholic and the rest nominal Protestant, it seemed an impossible request, for it was many years since any bright testimony of an evangelical nature had shone in the grey, dirty, riverside town where the world's greatest oceangoing liners had been built. Religious bigotry existed, Communism flourished alongside, and "Red Clydeside" hardly seemed a setting for a move of the Holy Spirit exalting the Name of the Savior.

Indeed, the fiery Irish evangelist W.P. Nicholson had shaken the dust from his feet there and abandoned an evangelistic campaign in protest against the extreme worldliness of the *clergy*. And, as if in condemnation from on high, Clydebank had soon lain in ruins after two air raids on consecutive nights in 1940, leaving 17,000 people dead and thousands more injured and homeless.

But God moves in mysterious ways. The young man who prayed over the city did not realize that I, his own brother, as yet unconverted, would become part of the answer to his prayer.

After my conversion, the stricture and confines of a Presbyterian church with unconverted minister and elders proved unbearable. And when the Lord met me with the baptism in His Holy Spirit, I had to find meaningful fellowship.

With a flock of four young people, I began to hold house meetings, in a day when it was not so common or fashionable as it is now. At the time, my family lived in two small rooms in a shared house, and I worked at a salesman's job with a meager salary. But I nourished an unquenchable conviction that God Himself had instituted the weekly house meeting to function as the Body of Christ.

The work grew slowly but steadily. Many who came were interested in the charismata, but not in the Cross. Constantly attentive to God for the proper emphasis, we knew that "without tongues a man might see the Lord," but "without holiness no man shall see the Lord." Purity before power was, I felt, God's rule. It weeded out those who were concerned with "spiritual kicks" but who shunned repentance, restitution, or any form of self-denial.

Soon the Spirit of God was challenging me to give up my regular job and launch out in faith. In Scotland, unlike many other countries, full-time Christian workers on a faith basis are few, and the Scottish temperament with its conservative tradition does not respond easily to anything outside the status quo. Nevertheless, the Lord wonderfully confirmed the call by exhortation and prophecy through His Word and through three spiritual giants whom I had come to know.

Before long, thirty to forty young people were cramming regularly into our fifteen-foot-square room to seek God. Moving the furniture out for the meeting and dealing with souls in the bathroom was a blessing to our hearts, but we saw it was time to trust God for a more adequate meeting place where we could meet to worship in a scripturally designated way.

Elders and deacons were appointed, none of whom were over thirty years of age, and a church was established on New Testament principles. Although the local Pentecostal church had failed to secure a lease for holding services within the local government buildings, the Lord enabled us to move into the Police Court a few weeks later as a temporary stopgap. Four years later, we still worship on Sunday mornings in this place, the only meeting we hold outside the house.

Asking, seeking God long and earnestly, I read the promise in II Sam. 7: "For thou, O Lord of hosts, God of Israel, hast revealed to thy servant saying, I will build thee an house." Could it be that this promise to David of old was God's answer to me hundreds of years later? When I discussed the matter with my wife, she confirmed that the Lord had spoken to her very clearly from the same verse a year earlier, and with such divine impression that she had noted it in her Bible at the time.

But why should He build us a house? Was it not true that churches had tried for land in the town and been refused because of the scarcity due to the great rebuilding programs necessary after the damage suffered from bombing during the war? God indicated clearly that there were enough churches laying desolate and empty in the town without the addition of another.

And so, we approached a Christian architect and asked him to design what would be the first house, as far as we knew, ever specifically planned for Gospel purposes. Land was made available on a good central site a few months after we began to seek it; only the minor detail of financing remained to be settled. If God had instituted the proceedings, surely He would supply that, too. Appeals, faith-and-hints methods would be out; it must be a divine transaction between us and God with no reliance whatsoever on any outside agency. The temptation to enlist human aid was pressing indeed, but for us it had to be like it was for Esther: "If I perish, I perish." We would rely on God alone.

Could the God of George Mueller act on our behalf as He had done for His servant in a day gone past? In taking up Elijah's mantle, Elisha affirmed that novelty was unnecessary, updated methods irrelevant, the real truth is not new—He who calls Himself Jehovah Jireh will provide if His conditions are fulfilled.

As we prayed, vital lessons quickly emerged. There would be no miraculous supply if we had the means to meet the need ourselves. Were our bankbooks baptized in the Spirit?

We live in a generation when many seem to receive *a* baptism, but not *the* baptism. "You shall receive power after that the Holy Ghost is come upon you." Power for what? To witness, lay hands on the sick? Yes, but, less appealing to the flesh, to be and to do what He desires of us.

A dire financial need arose. Settlement had to be made within a few days or legal action would be taken against us. Where was the God of Elijah?

A young couple with most of their house still unfurnished received an unexpected legacy. It arrived right on the deadline. They looked at the empty room, the need of chairs, carpets, curtains; they looked at the check for more money than they'd ever had before; they looked to God and saw that the legacy was His answer for the fellowship's need; they handed over the exact amount required, the whole sum.

Another young woman in London was out in faith, serving the Lord. She had prayed for a little secondhand Volkswagen, and out of the blue God sent a check for the amount she needed. She was another who had been baptized in the Spirit and was keen to hear His voice. The Master spoke quietly and indicated that four hundred miles away we were up against another financial crisis. Without any appeal from us, she sent the check, again for the exact amount we required.

Three weeks later, this young woman came to our opening meeting. I thanked her for her obedience to the Lord and testified about the blessing it brought to see God use her to answer our needs. How I rejoiced to hear that, hardly had she obeyed the voice of the Spirit, when the Lord sent in the amount she needed to purchase the car.

Soon three years will have passed since the opening meetings of the Scottish Christian Witness Team, conducted by Arthur Wallis, well-known author and minister of the Word at Fountain Trust meetings here in the United Kingdom. What has evolved? What direction are we taking?

To worship the Lord in Spirit and in truth is one of our priorities. To have a burden for souls as personal workers and in far-flung outreach is another. To have real missionary interest is a vital necessity for any New Testament church, and few churches in the land will exceed our per capita missionary offerings. Outreach projects have been organized and blessed of God where young people have joined with us, even from America and Europe, in evangelizing remote needy areas of our own land. Some have gone out to do evangelistic work from the Team in response to the need to give ourselves as well as our substance. As part of our outreach ministry I have been enabled to go to India, Czechoslovakia, and the United States, because we know that "without vision the people perish." What has evolved over about ten years is a compact group, maintained at around fifty saints who form the nucleus of the fellowship and workers. Many others come for fairly extensive or brief periods before orbiting out and sharing some of what they have learned in the midst.

The greatest thrust of our present activity is witnessing right here in Scotland. At first that might seem paradoxical. Isn't Scotland one of the very few countries to have received a genuine God-given revival in the past twenty-five years? Hasn't Scotland been blessed with a truly heaven-sent visitation from the Holy Spirit in mighty sovereign power? Yes, this has occurred more than once on the Isle of Lewis off the northwest coast. In spite of this, however, many remote and non-remote areas have a crying need for sound evangelistic outreach, sound doctrinal Bible teaching. And the young people are responding to it.

Conviction by the Spirit divests them of the affectation of the world in dress and manner. The "pop" or "hip" aspect of much of today's Christianity leaves them unimpressed. Discipline in prayer and reading of the Word are evident in practical matters like their willingness to submit to rule and authority, their desire to give generously for the financial support of missionary work, and to follow restraint in association with the opposite sex till God calls them together. Although most of our members are under thirty years of age, God has given a remarkable measure of maturity to those who seek Him with dedicated hearts.

If our ambition is only to be members of a cult—the house church cult, the tongues cult, or any other popular prevailing cult—then we must obey the cult's regulations or we lose face in the eyes of the other cult adherents. If, however, we desire to develop in the area into which God by His Spirit has brought us, then we are not interested in the status symbols so revered of men, but in obeying the Holy Ghost. And does He not give the Holy Spirit to those who obey Him? The rule, government, authority, as well as the ministries detailed by the apostles must function if the house church is to bear resemblance to its predecessor in the New Testament.

With so much to learn and seemingly so little to give, we realize that in the final reckoning we deal with a sovereign God who impresses us to cry with Jabez of old, "Oh that thou wouldst bless me indeed, and enlarge my coast, and that thine hand might be with me, and that thou wouldest keep me from evil, that it might not grieve me." Having been prompted so to cry, we yearn that the divine benediction might be the one Jabez experienced: "And God granted him that which he requested."

How I Became a New Testament Priest

Joseph Fulton, O.P.
with Pat King

May They tell me I'm becoming a cranky old man. It's because I can't bear change. I loved the Latin Mass, and now it's all but gone. This new Sunday Mass, this new liturgy, is the most painful, unattractive service I've ever been to in my life. Maybe I am cranky. I know I'm provoked by all those Catholics who seem to be enjoying the English Mass.

June I never cared for long hair or beards, When that first bearded lector appeared in the sacristy I told him, "Your're not going to go out and read the Scriptures in our church with that beard. It would be very upsetting to all those families who are trying to raise their children by good standards," Now our whole neighborhood is surrounded by the long-haired, bearded people called hippies. Everywhere I go I see them. Unbearable, really.

July I find the Lord in the Eucharist and I cling to Him. I love Him. Yet He is not real to me. I believe that Jesus lived, that He taught the way of love, that He laid down His life for what He believed. But I can't be sure that He rose again, that He's alive today. I wish I could be sure that Jesus is risen and heaven is real.

August 5th The priests of the diocese will be gathering at the seminary for a retreat. I suppose I must go. They say a Father McNutt will be there. That should be interesting. I knew him when he was a Dominican student.

August 26th Priest's retreat. Father McNutt and Father Twohy spoke on preaching. What amazed me is that both of these men have given such a testimony on the reality of Jesus. Once before, I heard a priest who knew the reality of Jesus like these men, only he was an Episcopalian, Father Dennis Bennett from St. Luke's Episcopal in Seattle.

It was strange how I met Father Bennett. About eight years before, I'd read how the young people in his church were going to prayer meetings in the middle of the week, enjoying themselves, finding the reality of Jesus, and praying in tongues. It sounded so peculiar I didn't think it would last, but then I heard it was still going on. Then one day a young man came to me about starting a club for hot-rodders; with this young man was another boy his age who was the most different looking person I'd ever encountered. He glowed—he radiated happiness. I found he went to the St. Luke prayer meetings. Right away I was worried that because this young man went to prayer meetings, he would do something awful, like pray aloud in my parlor. As the evening wore on and we shared his story, our friendship developed. Later on I went to his home, and he was very beautiful with me, just witnessing love and never forcing me to listen about tongues or prayer meetings. He seemed to sense that I didn't like new things or change, and that I was hard to move.

One day he called me and asked if I would like to meet his pastor, Father Bennett and his wife, Rita. Even though I said yes, I was afraid to go because I expected them to be weird. They turned out to be fine people, and I ended up sharing with them how I longed to find the reality of Jesus. Father Bennett spoke in tongues and our young host interpreted. Very beautiful. Father Bennett had said, "You can have this gift, and you can know the reality of Jesus. Just kneel down before you go to bed and ask for it. Surrender yourself." But I didn't. I would rather suffer than do anything different.

But now these two priests with their testimonies reminded me of Father Bennett. I greeted Father McNutt afterward and told him I was impressed. He said that he was a Catholic Pentecostal. "Well then," I said, "have you ever heard of Father Bennett?"

"Why, he's famous the world over," one said. "I'd like to meet him." So I did something that took a great deal of courage; I picked up the phone and invited an Episcopal priest to a Catholic priest's retreat.

August 27th Father Bennett shared with us today, and many of the priests received him well. This afternoon I was in the prayer room alone with him when a young priest came in and knelt down beside him and asked Father to pray for him. I thought, "Why didn't he ask me? Why should an Episcopalian priest pray for my own Catholic priest brother? There's something dreadfully lacking in my life. Father Bennett seems to know Jesus, and I don't. And my goodness, look at me! My own brother is in need and I'm sitting here doing nothing."

I felt so helpless and worthless. I tried to pray. My need was so great that I had to surrender myself to Jesus. I heard myself praying in a new tongue. It was embarrassing, and I tried to do it quietly. Later Father Bennett said, "Did you realize that you were praying in your tongue?" I said, "Well, I was?"

September I don't feel any different, but an amazing thing happened today. I was walking outside the church and two bearded long-haired people came by. I began talking to them. I invited them to church. *Then I hugged them.* I loved them. There seems to be in me a new power to love.

October 1st My eighth graders asked if they could have a guitar Mass. Of course I'd read of them and was horrified. I'd said that we'd never have one of those awful Masses in our church! Today I found myself saying, "Of course we'll have it."

October 4th The guitar Mass was beautiful. As I read the Mass prayers, the ones I'd always hated because they were in English, I realized something I'd never seen before—the Mass prayers were full of praise and thanksgiving. It came to me that my whole prayer life is changing. I've begun to pray in praise and thanksgiving without realizing it. At the end of Mass I did something I've never done before. I opened my arms to the eighth-grade children and said, "Praise the Lord."

October 7th I was asked to teach the Epistles of St. Paul. I've taught them for years, but to my surprise I found that it had all become a new book. All the words I had read before became alive. No longer was it a document, but a live, living book.

October 25th I've met some of the Pentecostal ministers of the area. I'm not afraid of them at all. We all seemed to love each other as Jesus fills our lives with His Spirit.

March I've been noticing the young people hanging around after Mass is over. It occurred to me that we'd have to revive our youth clubs, get an athletic and social program going. Instead, tonight they took me by the hand and led me to the parish hall and said they wanted a prayer meeting. I went along. They passed out some gospel hymnbooks they'd found. They wanted to sing, and they wanted me to read the Bible. They wanted to pray. Someone said, "Why not do this every Sunday after the evening folk Mass?"

September Some of the young people feel we should express our love for our brothers in some practical way. They want to start feeding the poor on Sunday afternoon. The ladies and the St. Vincent de Paul men will help them. The Lord has released a great Spirit of love in our church and community.

November Praise God that the parish hall is large. Over 250 are coming to the prayer meeting. Often someone will speak in a prophetic way what they have heard or learned from the Lord. These meetings are so filled with the joy of the Lord that we all begin praising the Lord spontaneously and praying in tongues in a beautiful angelic melody and harmony.

January I always did believe that there were miraculous healings at great shrines. I never thought to pray for healings, though. We nominal Christians weren't used to such things. If people were ill, we prayed with them; but we never expected them to be healed. Somehow we had lost the reality of what the Lord says. The difference is, now we really believe. Scripture tells us to lay hands on the sick, and now we take it at its word. At the prayer service, a woman gave a testimony and then praised and glorified the Lord for healing her of cancer.

June At the beautiful Sunday feed-in, we gave dinner to over 900 hungry people. It is the young long-haired members who help so faithfully.

October Some people consider it strange that of the four priests who help out in the parish, only one besides myself, Father DeDomenico, has had the outpouring of the Holy Spirit in his life. I don't believe in pressuring people, but in loving them the way they are. It is the Lord himself who teaches us and draws us and ministers unto us. As people want it, they will come. I do praise God for Father DeDomenico. He and a team of lay people and sisters have classes now, helping people go more deeply into the Word of God and preparing them for the Baptism in the Holy Spirit. Following the classes, many are baptized when hands are laid on them.

December It seems long ago that I was so lonely and in such doubt. Whenever I preach to church people, I try to make them understand that what is happening is not heretical in any way. The Pentecostal movement is the most orthodox thing in the world. It is the reality and truth of what we've always believed. It is the truth of our creed: that God the Father, God the Son, and God the Holy Spirit are real; and that they love us; and work in our lives; and that what the Bible says is true.

Though we are many, we are one body in union with Christ.

Romans 12:5

Catholic Prayer Communities

Joe Mallon

Throughout the history of Christianity, there have been Spirit-filled Christians. Today, thousands of Roman Catholic Pentecostals can attest to the fact that we are living in a new Pentecost.

Through Pope John XXIII's calling upon the church to pray for a renewal of Pentecost and as a result of the Holy Spirit's influence on the Vatican II Council, the church is also being called to this new Pentecost.

Many study and prayer groups, such as the Cursillo, Better World Movement, and various campus movements have emerged. About five years ago, some of these searching communities in Philadelphia, Pennsylvania began to experience revolutionary changes in their lives. At first, no one knew what was causing it, but today there are at least 3,000 Catholics in the archdiocese of Philadelphia who do. It is the baptism in the Holy Spirit.

There are many similarities between the workings of the Holy Spirit in the New Testament and in His pattern of work with the Catholic Pentecostal movement in Philadelphia. My own experience is a case in point.

Prior to my knowing the fullness of the Holy Spirit, I considered Christ to be an impersonal force, generating nothing that could hold my attention beyond the routine Sunday obligation. I approached Him in words while my heart was engaged in building a real estate career. But the Prodigy of prodigies continued after me, as He does after us all.

One afternoon an old friend, Frank Slattery, persuaded me to make a retreat. He called it Cursillo. During that retreat, lying in bed after a long day, I found myself trying to suppress a desire to go to the chapel. It was a cold January night, and I was tired, but finally went. I can remember saying to myself on the way that the talks given by the priests and the laymen were great, but if God expected me to become the kind of enthusiastic Christians they were, He would have to help me.

As I knelt in the chapel, asking for His help, I felt an intense love welling up within me. The words of the song, "God Is Love," began taking on significance, underlining God's love for me. As I began to accept that love, joy poured into me; tears ran down my face. God was not as impersonal as I had made Him out to be. With this new assurance, I acknowledged that all I had to do was trust Him. I was flooded with a great peace.

Shortly after this experience, I realized a new need to know all I could about Jesus, and I wanted to share Him with others. I began to get up early to pray and/or go to Mass. Prior to that experience, if any one had told me it would be possible for me to be thirsty for Christ, I would have thought him a bit out of reality.

A Cursillo workshop was held in Blackwood, New Jersey and Robert and Ann Donnell were among those who attended from the Philadelphia area. They had gone to learn more about helping others find Christ, and both were profoundly affected by the witness of the lay speaker, Ralph Martin, who talked about living life as the Gospel teaches, not worrying about tomorrow but putting complete trust in the Lord. I began to see a new light in their lives.

A couple of months later, Bob and I visited Father O'Callahan, who had also participated in the workshop. He explained that Ralph Martin was involved in the Catholic Pentecostal movement; we had never heard of it, but wanted to learn more. Father O'Callahan lent us a tape on the subject, and after hearing it, I realized that what it called the baptism in the Holy Spirit was what had happened to me during the Cursillo retreat. I had to find out more about this movement and what the Lord was going to do through it.

A number of people who had attended the Blackwood workshop were drawn together to discuss their seeking God's great gift. At one of their meetings, Sister Rose Mary Quinn, temporarily assigned to the Philadelphia area, prophesied that nothing overt was to be done about starting a Pentecostal movement in that city, but that we were to meet in small prayer groups. We received confirmation of the prophecy through a prayer community in North Attleboro, Massachusetts.

During one of our later meetings, we discussed the Scripture I Cor. 12-14. Why shouldn't twentieth century Christians know the same fullness of Christ's promise as the early church did? Before long, we encounted a book called *Catholic Pentecostals,* written by Kevin and Dorothy Ranaghan. A group of us met at the home of Mr. and Mrs. William Johnson to share our feelings about the book. Although we did not realize it at the time, that meeting was our first Catholic Pentecostal prayer meeting. We began to pray that the new Pentecost would come to our city.

In time, we were led to seek a public meeting place and to invite others to join with us. The night before our first scheduled open meeting, a paralyzing snowstorm struck the area. It seemed only common sense to call off the meeting. However, no one did, and thirty people showed up, most of them arriving from distant suburbs.

After reading Scripture from Isaiah 6:7,8, we prayed that Jesus would send His teacher to us. Later we learned that five days earlier, a dozen Spirit-filled people in Ann Arbor, Michigan, had prayed for two hours that the Pentecostal movement would come to Philadelphia. And a prophecy given during a prayer meeting at Catholic University said that a messenger would be sent to the Church at Philadelphia. It was Brother Pancratius, who arrived on January 12, thinking it would take him six months to find a Catholic Pentecostal prayer group, only to be invited to ours that very evening. Truly the Holy Spirit was working to bring us together.

Brother Pancratius' presence with us encouraged me to use my gift of prayer tongues for the first time in public. He interpreted, and there were many other manifestations of the Spirit that night. As the weeks passed, we sensed the new coming of the Holy Spirit to the Church in Philadelphia, in fulfillment of Rev. 3:7,8: "Write to the angel of the Church in Philadelphia and say, 'Here is the message of the holy and faithful one who has the key of David, so that when he opens, nobody can close, and when he closes, nobody can open: I know all about you; and now I have opened in front of you a door that nobody will be able to close.' " Because the Documents of

Vatican II stated that "No project may claim the name 'Catholic' unless it has obtained the consent of the lawful church authority," we were led to send a letter to the cardinal of our archdiocese regarding the movement in Philadelphia. Four days later, a reply from His Eminence John Cardinal Kroll was received, assigning Bishop Martin M. Lohmuller as liaison between his office and our prayer community.

Subsequently, the growth of the Catholic Pentecostal movement in Philadelphia has been tremendous. There are now over forty prayer communities of various sizes, numbering from groups of 2 or 3 (coffee klatches) to the larger prayer communities of 75 to 300. People from all walks of life and all ages are represented. Spin-off communities have been developed in neighboring dioceses, and members of our core community have helped develop new prayer communities throughout the Philadelphia area. Our pastoral team has conducted missions in other dioceses and we have also been called upon to give days of recollection to sisters and priests. Everywhere the gifts of the Spirit have been poured out.

The Documents of Vatican II further state: "From the reception of these charisms or gifts . . . there arise for each believer the right and duty to use them in the church and in the world . . . for the upbuilding of the church. In so doing, believers need to enjoy the freedom of the Holy Spirit who breathes where He wills. At the same time laymen must act in communion with their brothers in Christ, especially with their pastors. The latter must make a judgment about the true nature and proper use of these gifts, not in order to extinguish the Spirit, but to test all things and hold fast to what is good."   In the Philadelphia community, all the gifts mentioned in I Cor. 12-14 are present, especially in community. Those who have the gift of healing are aware that it is the Lord doing the healing, and that they are representative of the Body of Christ. The gift of tongues and interpretation of tongues is being exercised through children as well as adults, and such varied languages as French, German, Slovak, Ancient Greek, Greek, Russian, Hindu, Hebrew, and Arabic have been recognized. The gift of prayer tongues in the Philadelphia area seems to be normative with the baptism in the Holy Spirit, some 80 percent of the people involved in the movement in that area having the gift.

As our community and our pastoral team have grown, we are increasingly aware of the truth found in Romans 12:5: "Though we are many, we are one body in union with Christ and we are all joined to each other as different parts of one body." Over two years have seen our community evolve from rather simple beginnings to a movement embracing thousands of Catholics living in the archdiocese of Philadelphia. Many of the people who founded prayer communities started out from Saint Boniface Church; some came from other local churches. On January 13, 1972, leaders from the various prayer communities in the area met for a dinner at the Newman Center of the University of Pennsylvania, beginning the evening with a celebration of the Mass. Our prayer is that as our communities are united by the Holy Spirit, we may cooperate in teaching and spreading the Word of God, that the Spirit of Christ may flow abundantly through His Body here, and throughout the whole world.

The Pattern of the New Testament Church

Dennis Baker

Billy Graham was once accused of setting the church back fifty years. He replied with chagrin that he had hoped to set it back two thousand years. The authors of the preceding chapters about New Testament churches likewise possess the same hope. They have shared their stories in order that we might see how God has answered their prayers for New Testament reality in the church today.

The work of the Holy Spirit in the midst of the New Testament church is manifested in three distinct ways. First, or usually first, the gifts *(charismata)* and power uniquely available from the Spirit are experienced by the people. This draws them together into groups without regard for the usual religious and social boundaries, where the operation of the gifts and the love between them gives new depth of meaning to the old word "fellowship". Sometimes they even want to live in community together, share belongings, and allow others to correct or teach them in a way strongly reminiscent of the fellowship, or *koinonia,* of the first believers. And, the newly formed groups or communities of Spirit-baptized believers have a message to proclaim; testimonies that reach out to others in need of God. The early church referred to both the message and the outreach as *kerygma.*

CHARISMA: The Holy Spirit visited the people in the stories you have just read in 2,000 year-old ways—speaking in tongues, prophesying, and manifesting healing and other miracles. They no longer sit in pews thinking or saying, "I am rich, I have prospered, and I need nothing." They move from lukewarmness to a heated desire to know God.

They were people who saw they needed God. Once they sat in sodden lukewarmness, then they became acutely aware of their needs and began moving toward Jesus. The results speak eloquently enough. But, what happened to produce this change?

God's Word offers a clue. When some Greeks approached Philip about seeing Jesus, and Philip and Andrew spoke to Jesus about it, they were given what seemed to be an enigmatic answer: "The hour has come for the son of man to be glorified," Jesus said. "Truly, truly, I say to you, unless a grain of wheat falls into the earth and dies, it remains alone; but if it dies, it bears much fruit." (John 12: 23-24) What did that have to do with Jesus meeting with some Greeks?

The relevance of Jesus' remarks is seen in retrospect. He was referring to the ancient mystery (Eph. 3:6) that included the Greeks (Gentiles) in the covenant community. They would indeed be able to "see Jesus" but only his death and resurrection, not an interview, would make it possible.

Death and resurrection are more than a one time occurrence in the founding of a New Testament church. Involved is a principle which applies to all those who follow Jesus, in every age. Dying to self produces new life, a revival in the Spirit; the stirring and refreshing of dry bones in the valley.

The experience of Bob Hooley of Denver, Colorado is a good example. A successful California businessman, Bob's particular world was shaken by the misery of his wife Carol, who was afflicted with a crippling back ailment. At a meeting of the Full Gospel Business Men's Fellowship one night, Carol was healed instantly. Overwhelmed by this act of God's mercy, Bob sold his share of his business and moved to Denver to start a church.

He invested what funds he had in an apartment house, housed his family in it, and supported them with the rental income. He then set out with great zeal to preach the gospel. After several months when nothing spiritually rewarding had happened, a deeply disappointed Bob cried out to God for an explanation. He received this word: "Sell the apartment house, willingly invest the funds in my work, and learn to depend entirely on me."

Should he throw away security in order to establish another church in a city that already had plenty? Bob Hooley died a little to desires of self and flesh, abandoned his former plan, and in faith stepped out of one way of life into another. Today, Faith Bible Chapel stands in the midst of Denver's inner city, its huge auditorium overflowing several times a week with enthusiastic worshipers and disciples. Bob paid the price that God required and found himself no longer alone. Other people came to life when he died to his own plans and did things God's way.

Whenever a Christian cries for an outpouring of the Spirit in his congregation or community, God will want to know if he is willing to pay the price of being a kernel of wheat, falling into the ground to die in order that others might come to life. Dying for one's congregation or community could take many forms. Sometimes the death is literal. Always the death embraces our love of self and our desire to go our own way.

KOINONIA: Many translators today are reluctant to render this word in its usual form—*fellowship*—because the average reader is likely to associate it with box lunch socials and coffee after, or between, services. Actually the term has a different connotation. It is related to words like community and communion.

The *koinonia* of the early church was expressed by a form of community both spiritual and economic. Among the first believers, there were no rulers to lord it over the others. All possessed the Spirit and exercised gifts and ministries for the benefit of the others. Even the women were full participants, admitted to the prayer room and communion table along with the men. They also shared their possessions, as well as their supernatural gifts, delighting to help the poor among themselves and in the neighborhood about them.

Vaughan Rees tells, in his book *The Jesus Family in Communist China* (CLC, 1970), of a modern group of Chinese Christians who formed themselves into a commune during the 1930's. The first year of their operation they gave away a tenth of their income to support poor families living nearby. The second year they increased the amount of their charitable gifts to equal twenty percent of their income. At the end of ten years their trust in God had grown to the point that they were giving away one hundred percent of their funds and food.

When the Communist regime was established in China after

World War II, the government wanted to do away with the commune but had difficulty finding an excuse to do so. Commissars would harrass the community from time to time with inspection tours, but to no avail.

In their life of *koinonia,* the Chinese believers applied Jesus' precept that to be great in the church one must be the servant of his brethren, and to be ranked first among them one must be their slave (Matt. 20:20-28). Their leaders made it a point to take upon themselves the lowliest and most unwanted tasks of the community. One day some commissars arrived and demanded to see the leader. They expected to meet some grand personage but no one like that appeared. Then a man approached them pushing a wheelbarrow full of rank manure. He stopped in front of them and the commissars backed away holding their noses. "Yes, I am the leader. What do you want?" he asked. The Communists were speechless.

Koinonia, that life into which the Spirit of God draws us to be together in Christ, has a marvellous effect on those who experience it. The atmosphere of togetherness is especially suited to provoking and sustaining change in the members. Personality defects, and immaturities hidden in previous relationships, begin to come to the surface for final eradication. We come to see ourselves with increasing clarity and frankness. We cry out for Jesus to make us truly new creatures.

In such a company of believers, there is a peculiar sense in which the lamb of God meets us as the lion of Judah. We can begin to admit we can be wrong because we are both loved and pressed to desperation by close contact with the brethren. It is an ability to be coveted by every Christian. After the successful siege of Vicksburg in 1863, President Lincoln sent a letter of congratulation to General Grant. The message closed with a frank admission by Lincoln that earlier he had thought Grant was mistaken for not joining forces with another Union General before encircling Vicksburg. He concluded:

"I now wish to make the personal acknowledgment that you were right, and I was wrong.

Yours very truly,
A. Lincoln."[1]

The freedom to be wrong and willing to change is one of the surest signs of maturity in any person. As we become members of a spiritual fellowship, God moves to break down the two greatest obstacles to our discipleship, self-righteousness and self-justification. When we have the capacity to confess or admit our errors, then we can meet others without defensiveness. We can be clear channels through which the love of God can flow.

KERYGMA: Students of group dynamics have noted that a group, if it is to prosper, cannot continually turn inward but must reach outside itself as well. The inward thrust of the church is its koinonia, or fellowship; the outward thrust is its kerygma — *proclamation.*

The church's mission has been neglected in these first years of the charismatic renewal. True, there has been generous financial support for overseas and domestic mission work in places where the Holy Spirit has been poured out, and men have opened themselves to the dealings of God. But in comparison to the great revivals of days past—the charismatic movement in the historic denominations is still a pale horse.

One great obstacle to missionary outreach has been the attitude of the denominations themselves. The pronouncements of their headquarters speak frequently of the passing of the traditional missionary. To be accepted by denominational mission boards today, the candidate must be an engineer, a pilot, an agricultural expert, or a medical specialist.

Since most of the people in the charismatic movement are members of traditional churches, it is understandable that they might believe missionary work is something reserved for the elite few. This combined with the Holy Spirit's emphasis on the koinonia aspects of church life, has produced a visible decline in volunteers for missionary service.

But, as one old-time missionary put it, "God is never in a hurry, and he is never late." The need for missionaries is greater than ever and there is evidence that God is preparing a core group of men and women for missionary service. The Jesus people were never accused of lacking missionary zeal; today many of them are in some kind of training (not infrequently involving communal living) which will prepare them for the mission field. In addition there are instances of men in early middle-age who are preparing to leave or have already left lucrative jobs to depend on God as they undergo intensive preparation for new careers of service in the Kingdom of God.

Ron was one of the Jesus people. He had met Christ in Iran while traveling the Marseilles to Afghanistan hippie trail. Ron's walk with Christ was unsteady but there was no gainsaying his enormous enthusiasm for Jesus. After a spell in an Irish jail, he found himself back in the States where he tried to settle into a New Testament church and hold down a regular job. It was like bringing a wild stallion into a tiny corral—several times he was tempted to leap the fence when the urge to return to international roving came upon him.

In his New Testament church, Ron was loved during these bad moments and taught how to deal with them. He learned about for-giveness, submission to delegated authority, and about getting rid of ancient bitterness. He responded positively to tender-loving-care and teaching; he even shaved his beard and cut his hair, things he had retained to go back into street society with if Jesus didn't work out.

Ron has since submitted himself to the intense discipline of a Christian community in which the participants have mutually pledged to correct one another in love, and in turn be open to correction. The severity of such a life pierces deep into a man's spirit and brings much to the surface that might otherwise re-main hidden.

It is of God's mercy to deal with Ron in this intensified type of fellowship. Uneven spiritual growth and hidden conflicts would sabotage Ron on the mission field where he hopes to serve his Savior, but the closeness of *koinonia* will produce a man truly prepared to preach the Gospel even under pressure.

Bill was nearly a millionaire when he met Christ. His financial counsel to professional men had brought him into demand through-out his home town. He lived with his attractive wife and children in a spacious suburban home. After their conversion at a Faith At Work conference, they became active in a church where par-ticipation in small group meetings brought them into contact with Spirit-filled people. It was not long until Bill and Jane were speaking in tongues, raising their hands in worship and praying for a real move of God in their community. Their home became a meeting place for Spirit-baptized teenagers seeking counsel and encouragement. God was moving, and the thrill and surge of it all brought a whole new dimension to Bill and Jane's life.

Then opposition to their "revival" caused Bill and Jane to leave their suburban church to join a large New Testament assembly. Bill believed the Lord was telling him to discontinue his financial counseling and to begin to wait upon the Lord in prayer and fasting. Subsequently, he vacated his office and began to face the humiliation that came every time someone asked him what he did for a living. Bill learned to give up the desire to be understood. He and the family began to trust God to provide their needs more openly than ever before.

He spent some of his free days with a dying alcoholic who lived in an inner-city flat. Bill would daily bring groceries, cook, clean, and care for the helpless old man, who was so bitter that he could hardly bear to hear Bill speak of Christ. And for several months Bill also visited hospital patients with incurable diseases.

Recently, his pastor and elders counselled him to get a regular job. Bill had already been listening to the Holy Spirit speak to the same point and, encouraged by this confirmation, took a job with a janitorial firm.

Why did God lead Bill along a path from riches to rags? It is easy to see that a man who had every reason to be proud of his accomplishments had humbled himself—even emptied himself— counting his many accomplishments as nothing that he might win Christ. But, more specifically, Bill had undergone previous conflicts with his unconverted parents and it was especially important for him to learn to humble himself before them.

Out of this crushing, a sweet savor is arising from Bill's life, a new man is being born—a man increasingly equipped for every good work. And there are many more like Bill who are being quietly prepared behind the scenes—nurtured in the koinonia that they might effectively give forth kerygma.

Conclusion: It is impossible to separately define and discuss *charisma, koinonia,* and *kerygma.* They are a unity and a progression: a unity in the sense that each one functions completely in the context of the other, and that there is no clear point of departure where one ends and another begins; a progression because the outpouring of the Holy Spirit brings forth a community which in turn proclaims that Jesus has been raised from the dead and that he is Lord of all.

The sure sign that a church is functioning according to New Testament standards is not the presence of the gifts of the spirit, nor anointed preaching alone; nor is it necessarily the presence of apostles, prophets, evangelists, teachers and pastors, nor even the performance of miracles. However important the restoration of these things to the life of the Church, nothing is more of a hallmark of biblical authenticity than the presence of an individual and corporate willingness to pass repeatedly through the cycles of life, death and resurrection—through the process of *charisma, koinonia,* and *kerygma.*

¹Bruce Catton, Grant Moves South (Boston: Little, Brown and Company, 1960), p. 489

SUGGESTED INEXPENSIVE PAPERBACK BOOKS
WHEREVER PAPERBACKS ARE SOLD
OR USE ORDER FORM.

BEN ISRAEL by Arthur Katz
with Jamie Buckingham A503/95¢ -
Odyssey of a modern Jew and
his search for the Messiah.

THE ARMSTRONG ERROR by Charles DeLoach L317/95¢
A reporter investigates Herbert W. Armstrong, The World Tomorrow
broadcast, and the Plain Truth movement.

LOST SHEPHERD by Agnes Sanford L328/95¢
First time in paperback after 7 printings in hard cover. The accounts
of a minister's search for a dynamic ministry and a woman with an
unconventional healing ministry.

AGLOW WITH THE SPIRIT
by Dr. Robert Frost L326/95¢
A scientist shows his spiritual discovery of the baptism in the
Holy Spirit.

WALK IN THE SPIRIT by Michael Harper L319/95¢
There is a place where there is a life to live through the Holy Spirit.

COMING ALIVE by Jamie Buckingham A501/95¢
YOUR NEW LOOK by Jamie Buckingham A502/95¢
COMING ALIVE is a book written for parents and children of pre-
junior high level, presenting a Christian view of sex information.
YOUR NEW LOOK is for the junior high age-level.

15 STEPS OUT by Bob Mumford L106/1.50
Vital questions of practical living considered in relation
to Psalms 120-134.

OVERFLOWING LIFE by Robert Frost L327/1.75
The exciting fulfillment of a spirit-filled life. The experiences
expected after the baptism in the Holy Spirit.

THE SOUL PATROL by Bob Bartlett A500/95¢
A gripping account of teen challenge in Philadelphia, its birth
and outreach to addicts, dropouts and problem youth.

BORN TO BURN by Wendell Wallace with Pat King A508/95¢
Pastor of a multi-racial church
Speaks out on the issues today.

PSEU-DO CHRISTIANS by Dr. Ray Jarman A516/95¢
The dangers of liberal and occult
teaching in lives of Christians and non-Christians.
Dr. Jarman for 50 years was a leader in science of the mind
religions until a dramatic conversion at 70 years of age.

THIS EARTH'S END by Carmen Benson A513/95¢
The Bible contains prophecy telling how this earth
will end. This is a clearly written, easy to understand
explanation of dreams and visions in the New Testament.

JESUS AND ISRAEL by Carmen Benson A514/95¢
The Old Testament revealed through dreams and visions
the future happenings on the earth. An accurate account
of things to come.

WALK IN THE SPIRIT by Michael Harper L319/95¢
Renewal or Revolution — The Church must decide. Some have
discovered a new dimension in living through God's power.

GONE IS SHADOW'S CHILD by Jessie Foy L337/95¢
A moving story of a mother's faith in God for
her son and of a highly effective B10-chemical
treatment called megavitamin in schizophrenia.

SPIRITUAL WARFARE A505/95¢
A practical study on demon oppression and exorcism.
A positive method in freeing the oppressed.

GOD'S JUNKIE by Sonnie Arguinzoni
with Jouinn Ricketts A509/95¢
Introduction by David Wilkerson
A former junkie (his story is in Run Baby Run)
tells of the unique addict church — "Miracles do
happen" by Nicky Cruz.

HEAR MY CONFESSION by Fr. Joseph E. Orsini
L341/95¢ A Roman Catholic priest tells his
personal story of how he discovered the Catholic
Pentecostal experience.

THERE'S MORE L344/1.50

RUN BABY RUN by Nicky Cruz L-101/95¢
The true story of a gang leader turned crusader.

THE LONELY NOW by Nicky Cruz
with Jamie Buckingham A510/95¢
Nicky answers the questions youth ask.